DIY
Wrap Bracelets

DIY Wrap Bracelets
First published in the English language by Fons & Porter Books, an imprint of
F+W, a Content + eCommerce Company, 10151 Carver Road, Suite 200, Blue Ash,
Ohio 45242. (800) 289-0963. First Edition.

media
www.fwmedia.com

Original Japanese edition published by Nihon Vogue Co., LTD. in the following title:
HANDMADE DE OSHARENA BRACELET BOOK (NV80340)
Copyright © Keiko Sakamoto/NIHON VOGUE-SHA 2013

English language rights, translation & production by Wolrd Book Media, LLC
Email: info@worldbookmedia.com
Photographers: Yukari Shirai and Noriaki Moriya
Translator: Kyoko Matthews
English-language editors: Judith Durant and Lindsay Fair

Distributed in Canada by Fraser Direct
100 Armstrong Avenue
Georgetown, ON, Canada L7G 5S4
Tel: (905) 877-4411

Distributed in the U.K. and Europe by F&W MEDIA INTERNATIONAL
Brunel House, Newton Abbot, Devon, TQ12 4PU, England
Tel: (+44) 1626 323200, Fax: (+44) 1626 323319
Email: enquiries@fwmedia.com

Distributed in Australia by Capricorn Link
P.O. Box 704, S. Windsor NSW, 2756 Australia
Tel: (02) 4560 1600, Fax: (02) 4577 5288
E-mail: books@capricornlink.com.au

SRN: T8258
ISBN-13: 978-1-4402-4473-5

19 18 17 16 15   5 4 3 2 1
Manufactured in China

DIY
Wrap Bracelets

28 DESIGNS using beads, thread, charms, ribbon, cord and more

Keiko Sakamoto

Fons&Porter

CONTENTS

Before You Begin

Tools...**6**

Materials...**7**

Wrap Jewelry

Square Bead Wrap Bracelets...**14**

Ocean Mist Necklace & Hoop Earrings...**16**

Nautical Wrap Bracelets...**18**

Sparkling Chiffon Bracelet & Necklace...**20**

Simple Wrap Bracelets...**22**

Technique Overview: The Ladder Stitch...**23**

Friendship Jewelry

Linen Charm Bracelets...**42**

Braided Friendship Bracelets...**43**

Braided Seed Bead Bangle...**44**

Woven Fabric Bracelets...**45**

Beaded Square Knot Bracelet...**46**

Square Knot Rope Amulets...**47**

Doubled Rope Bracelet...**48**

Convertible Braid Bracelets...**49**

Technique Overview:

    The Five-Strand Braid...**50**

    The Four-Strand Round Braid...**53**

    The Square Knot Rope...**55**

Classic Jewelry

Turquoise Bracelets...**72**

Wire Work Bracelets...**73**

Cotton Pearl Bracelets & Long Necklace...**74**

Champagne Pearl Set...**76**

Beaded Brooch Bracelet...**78**

Technique Overview: The Wrapped Loop...**80**

Global Jewelry

Winding Wire Bracelets & Choker...**104**

Wave Bracelets...**106**

Woven Bead Cuffs...**107**

Crystal Wrapped Bangles...**108**

Wrap Bracelet Tips & Tricks

Bracelet Combinations...**120**

Simple Wrap Bracelets...**122**

Jewelry Making Technique Guide...**124**

Tools

Round-nose pliers
Use the round tips to curl wires and pins.

Flat-nose pliers
Use the flat tips to squeeze crimp beads and cord ends closed.

Wire cutters
Use the sharp tips to cut through wire.

Beading needles
Larger than standard sewing needles, beading needles are specially designed to string beads onto thread.

Jeweler's awl or crochet hook
Use a narrow, pointed instrument for manipulating small, detailed areas.

Scissors
Use to trim thread and cord.

Materials

STRINGING MATERIALS

Embroidery floss
Available in a wide variety of colors and weights, embroidery floss is perfect for making friendship bracelets.

Leather cord
Strong and stiff, leather cord is ideal for knotting and braiding. Round leather cord is commonly used throughout this book.

Hemp string
Made from 100% hemp, this natural fiber cord has the perfect texture for friendship bracelets.

Monofilament cord
Specifically designed for bead-work, use this lightweight cord when ladder stitching beads to leather cord.

Beading thread
This thread is thin enough to string seed beads, yet firm enough to not require the use of a beading needle.

FINDINGS

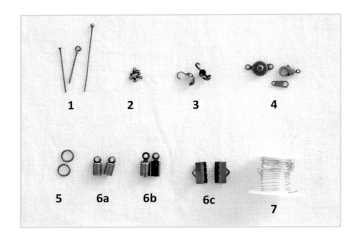

1. Headpins and eyepins: String beads onto a pin to create a hanging element or to connect other beads. Pins are available in a variety of sizes and styles. Some pins even feature design elements such as loops and balls.

2. Bead crimps: Use pliers to squeeze a bead crimp closed, creating a secure and professional finish for your beadwork.

3. Bead tips: Use bead tips to create secure connections to jump rings and clasps.

4. Clasps: Secure your jewelry in place while being worn. Refer to page 11 for more information on selecting the best clasp for your project.

5. Jump rings: Used to connect various jewelry components.

6. Cord ends: Cover the ends of cord, allowing the cord to attach to a clasp or other component. There are several different types:

   a. Apply glue inside this type of cord end, then insert the cord.
   b. This style wraps around the end of the cord. Use pliers to squeeze the side tabs closed around the cord.
   c. Use this style to finish wide cords, such as ribbon or flat leather cord.

7. Wire: String beads onto wire for delicate jewelry designs.

Jump ring

Jump ring

Close-up view of jump rings being used to attach a metal charm to the Wire Work Bracelet shown on page 73.

BEADS

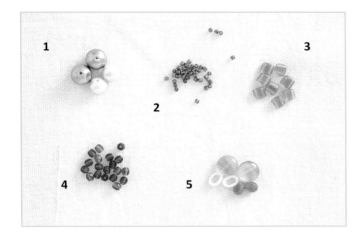

1. Cotton pearls: Made from compressed cotton and covered with a pearl coating, this type of bead is much lighter than a traditional pearl.

2. Seed beads: As their name suggests, seed beads are small glass beads that resemble seeds. Seed beads are available in an extensive range of colors.

3. Czech glass beads: Available in a variety of shapes, these beads are made in the Czech Republic.

4. Fire-polished beads: Often made in the Czech Republic, these beads undergo a polishing process in which the surface is melted to create a smooth, shiny finish.

5. Gemstones: Made from natural materials, such turquoise and quartz, these beads are often associated with healing properties.

Close-up view of Czech glass beads strung onto leather cord for the Square Bead Wrap Bracelet shown on page 14.

CHARMS

Decorative charms often serve as the focal point of a bracelet design. You can string charms directly onto the cord or hang them from pins and jump rings. Jewelry connectors are a functional type of charm that join multiple strands together.

OTHER COMPONENTS

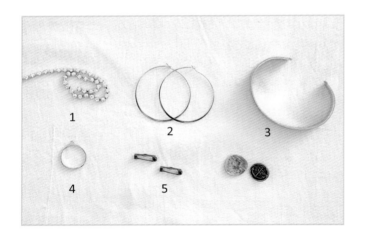

1. Cupchain: This lightweight, flexible chain is composed of rhinestones in prong settings. Use this material to add a bit of sparkle to your jewelry designs.

2. Earring bases: String beads directly onto wire hoops or attach beaded pins.

3. Bangle bracelet base: Cover this metal bracelet form with beads, fabric, or thread.

4. Ring base: Design your own rings to complement the various bracelet designs in this book.

5. Pin backs: Create beaded brooches using simple pin backs.

6. Buttons: Large, decorative buttons are perfect to use as bracelet clasps.

SELECTING THE CLASP

The clasp is a very important component of jewelry making. In addition to serving an important function, clasps also influence the overall look of your design. Since bracelets are worn around the wrist, their clasps are often visible, so choose a style that works well with the other elements of your design.

BUTTON CLASPS

These clasps are created by forming one end of the bracelet into a loop and attaching a button to the other. Vintage clothes are an excellent source for the type of large, decorative buttons used for clasps.

Hammered metal or rhinestone buttons add a bit of texture and sparkle

Wood and shell buttons work well with casual, rustic bracelet designs

TOGGLE CLASPS

This style of clasp is composed of a ring and a bar. Hook the bar through the ring to close the clasp. Often made of metal, toggle clasps are available in a variety of finishes.

Toggle clasps are available in both simple and ornate styles

METAL CLASPS

Secure and easy to fasten, metal clasps are the most popular type of jewelry closure. If possible, opt for high quality metal, such as 14K gold-plate, for professional-looking jewelry that will last for years to come.

There are several varieties of metal clasps available

METAL CLASP VARIATIONS

 Button Clasp: This type of clasp snaps closed and is recommended for bracelets since it is easily fastened with one hand.

 Spring Clasp: Pull the tab to open the clasp, then hook it into the corresponding ring.

 Lobster Clasp: Named for its resemblance to a lobster claw, this clasp operates in the same manner as the spring clasp.

1.

Wrap Jewelry

Wrap bracelets are the perfect balance of trendy style and laid-back cool. This section features popular leather wrap bracelets plus versatile designs that can convert from long necklaces into wrap bracelets. Also included are coordinating necklaces and earrings designed to complement the wrap bracelets.

Square Bead Wrap Bracelets

This triple wrap bracelet showcases flat, square beads.
Experiment with different colors of leather cord and
beads to create a variety of styles.

Instructions on page 23

Insert the button through the knotted leather cord to fasten this wrap bracelet.

When worked in a darker color scheme, this bracelet is also suitable for men.

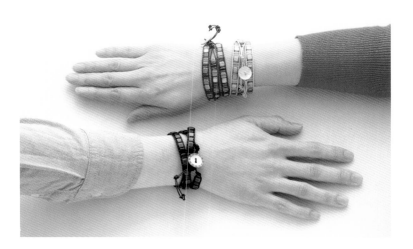

Ocean Mist Necklace & Hoop Earrings

Inspired by the colors of the ocean, this jewelry set makes a wonderful gift. The necklace and earrings are quick and easy to make, and the bracelet is a blue variation of the Square Bead Wrap Bracelet shown on page 14.

Instructions on page 27

For a casual, yet stylish look, wear two pieces from the set, such as the bracelet and necklace.

Nautical Wrap Bracelets

A   B

The nautical-inspired brass charms are the focal points of these beaded bracelets. Use a single color for the beads, or combine similar shades for a subtly variegated look. This versatile design can also be worn as a long necklace.

Instructions on page 30

4

Sparkling Chiffon Bracelet & Necklace

Braid rhinestone chain with strips of chiffon fabric to create this shabby chic wrap bracelet. Combine the same braid technique with metallic beads for this elegant multi strand necklace.

Instructions on page 34

With its sparkly rhinestones, this bracelet works well for both casual and formal occasions.

Use a toggle clasp for a simple, yet stylish bracelet closure.

Simple Wrap Bracelets

These double wrap bracelets feature gemstone-inspired Czech glass beads. Experiment with different colors for the beads, cord, and thread to create unlimited variations of this classic wrap bracelet.

Instructions on page 39

Wrap Jewelry Technique Overview

THE LADDER STITCH

As its name suggests, the ladder stitch is used to join beads together in a ladder-like pattern. This technique can be used with a variety of different beading materials.

The following guide uses the blue variation of the Square Bead Wrap Bracelet shown on page 14 as an example. Use the same technique for all variations.

Square Bead Wrap Bracelets

Shown on page 14

MATERIALS

Refer to pages 25 and 26 for color combinations and bead patterns for each bracelet variation.

▸ 6 mm square Czech glass beads
▸ One ⅝" (15 mm) shell button
▸ 59" (150 cm) of 1.2 mm round leather cord
▸ 138" (350 cm) of nylon beading thread

TOOLS

▸ Beading needle
▸ Jeweler's awl

FINISHED SIZE

▸ 24 ¾" (63 cm) long

As a general rule, make wrap bracelets triple your desired finished size when worn on the wrist.

INSTRUCTIONS

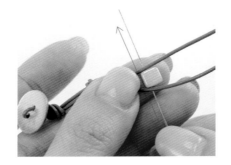

Center of leather cord

⅝" (1.5 cm)

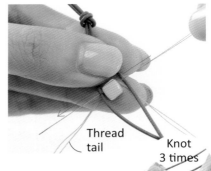

Thread tail

Knot 3 times

1. String the shell button onto the center of the leather cord. Make an overhand knot (see page 96) right after the button, then make another knot ⅝" (1.5 cm) away.

2. Thread a single strand of beading thread onto the needle. Holding the bead between the two leather cords, pass through the first set of holes in the bead, keeping the needle under the cords and leaving a 6" (15 cm) long thread tail.

3. Turn the needle around and pass back through the same set of holes, keeping the needle over the leather cords this time. Knot the thread and thread tail together 3 times.

> **Note:** Always remember to keep the thread under the leather cords on the first pass, then over the leather cords on the second pass.

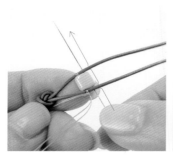

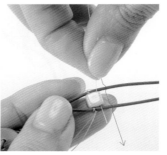

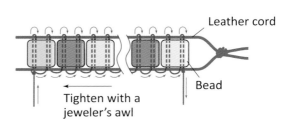

Leather cord

Bead

Tighten with a jeweler's awl

4. Follow the same process to insert the thread through the second set of holes in the bead. Follow the same process to string all 77 beads. Refer to page 25 for bead pattern.

> **Note:** Nylon beading thread is easily loosened, so use a jeweler's awl to periodically tighten the thread as you work.

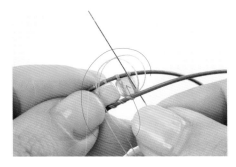

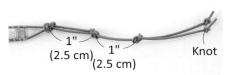

1" (2.5 cm)   1" (2.5 cm)   Knot

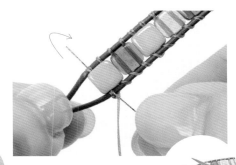

5. After stringing the last bead, knot the thread 3 times by bringing the thread under the leather cord as indicated by the arrow. Pass the thread back through the last 2 or 3 beads, then trim the excess.

6. Knot the doubled leather cord 3 times (position the knots as desired in order to adjust the bracelet's length). Knot the ends of the two strands of cord individually.

7. Thread the beginning tail onto the needle. Pass the thread back through the first bead, then trim the excess.

BEAD PATTERN

BLUE VARIATION

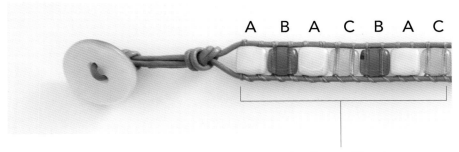

A B A C B A C

A: Ivory = 33 beads
B: Blue = 22 beads
C: Clear Gray = 22 beads
Leather Cord: Blue
Nylon Beading Thread: Blue

1 pattern = 7 beads
Repeat this pattern 11 times

COLOR COMBINATIONS & BEAD PATTERNS

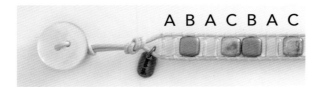

A B A C B A C

A: Clear Pink = 33 beads
B: Matte Gold = 22 beads
C: Iridescent Blue = 22 beads
Leather Cord: White
Nylon Beading Thread: White

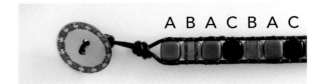

A B A C B A C

A: Metallic Blue = 33 beads
B: Clear Blue = 22 beads
C: Black = 22 beads
Leather Cord: Black
Nylon Beading Thread: Black

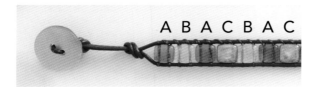

A B A C B A C

A: Clear Purple = 33 beads
B: Clear Pink = 22 beads
C: Iridescent Blue = 22 beads
Leather Cord: Red
Nylon Beading Thread: Red

A B A C B A C

A: Clear Turquoise = 33 beads
B: Clear Green = 22 beads
C: Matte Lime Green = 22 beads
Leather Cord: Black
Nylon Beading Thread: Gray

A B A C B A C

A: Clear Yellow = 33 beads
B: Clear Gold = 22 beads
C: Matte Gold = 22 beads
Leather Cord: Brown
Nylon Beading Thread: Brown

Ocean Mist Necklace & Hoop Earrings

Shown on page 16

FINISHED SIZE

- Earrings: About 1 ½" (3.5 cm) tall
- Necklace: About 15" (38 cm) long (up to 2 ½" [6 cm] longer with extender chain)

Refer to pages 23-25 for bracelet instructions.

MATERIALS

Earrings

- 6 mm square Czech glass beads
  - 4 ivory
  - 4 clear gray
  - 6 blue
- 28 brass 5 mm donut-shaped spacer beads
- Two brass ball-shaped end caps
- One pair of brass 1" (2.5 cm) diameter hoop earring bases with rubber earnuts
- Jewelry and bead glue

Necklace

- 6 mm square Czech glass beads
  - 5 ivory
  - 6 clear gray
  - 4 blue
- 20 brass 5 mm donut-shaped spacer beads
- Two brass 13 mm tube-shaped spacer beads
- 18 brass 0.7 x 30 mm headpins
- Two brass 4.5 mm jump rings
- Two brass cord ends
- One brass lobster clasp
- 2 ½" (6 cm) of brass extender chain
- 15" (38 cm) of 1.2 mm round turquoise leather cord

TOOLS

- Round-nose pliers
- Flat-nose pliers
- Wire cutters

INSTRUCTIONS

Earrings

1. String the beads onto the earring bases.

2. Glue an end cap onto each earring.

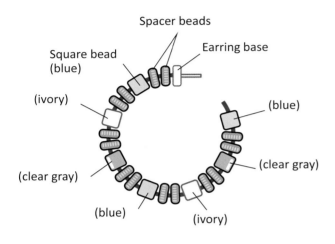

Spacer beads

Square bead (blue)

Earring base

(ivory)

(blue)

(clear gray)

(clear gray)

(blue)

(ivory)

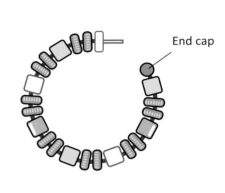

End cap

Necklace

1. For each part, string the beads onto two head-pins. Cut the excess wire and use round-nose pliers to curl the tips into loops.

Refer to the Jewelry Making Technique Overview on pages 124-125 for detailed instructions on making headpin loops.

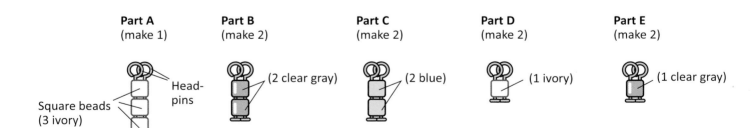

Part A
(make 1)

Head-pins

Square beads
(3 ivory)

Part B
(make 2)

(2 clear gray)

Part C
(make 2)

(2 blue)

Part D
(make 2)

(1 ivory)

Part E
(make 2)

(1 clear gray)

2. String the headpin loops and spacer beads onto the leather cord following the diagram below. Attach the cord ends, jump rings, lobster clasp, and extender chain.

Refer to the Jewelry Making Technique Guide on pages 124-125 for detailed instructions on attaching cord ends and jump rings.

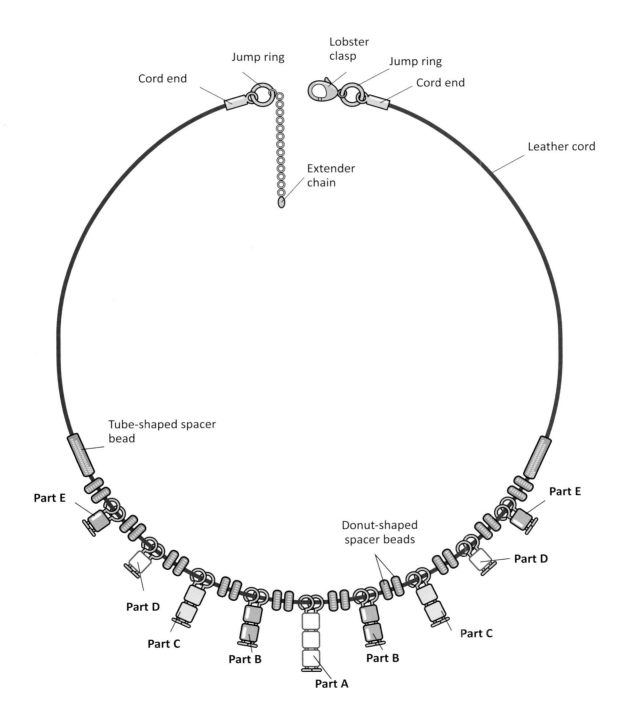

Nautical Wrap Bracelets

Shown on page 18

A   B

FINISHED SIZE

▸ About 39 ½" (100 cm) long

MATERIALS

Refer to the Color Combination Chart for colors and quantities for each bracelet variation.

▸ 150 4 mm round Czech glass beads
▸ One 6 mm faceted round Swarovski crystal bead
▸ 205 round seed beads
▸ One brass ¾" x 1" (20 x 25 mm) charm
▸ One brass 0.7 x 20 mm headpin
▸ Six brass 4.5 mm jump rings
▸ Two brass crimp beads
▸ 55" (140 cm) of pearl cotton #5 thread
▸ One magnetic clasp

TOOLS

▸ Beading needle
▸ Flat-nose pliers
▸ Round-nose pliers
▸ Wire cutters

COLOR COMBINATION CHART

	A	B
Round beads	50 white 50 light beige 50 pearlescent cream	150 blue gray
Swarovski crystal bead	Mocca	Indicolite
Seed beads	Metallic brown	Metallic brown
Brass charm	Yacht	Anchor
Embroidery floss	Light smoke brown	Light smoke blue

INSTRUCTIONS

1. Using a beading needle, string the first few beads, the crimp bead, and one half of the magnetic clasp onto a 55" (140 cm) long piece of pearl cotton #5 thread.

2. Squeeze the crimp bead flat using flat-nose pliers.

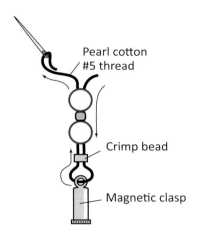

Pearl cotton
#5 thread

Crimp bead

Magnetic clasp

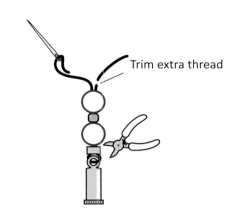

Trim extra thread

> **Note:** *You will use the same process on the other end of the bracelet once all the beads have been strung.*

How to Tie a Knot Flush to a Bead

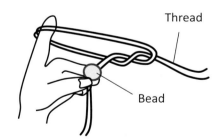

Thread

Bead

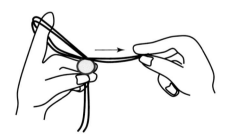

1. Tie an overhand knot and insert your left index finger into the loop.

2. Use your right hand to pull the thread tail and tighten the loop while keeping your left index finger in place.

3. Slowly remove your left index finger from the loop. Pull the thread tail to move the knot flush to the bead.

3. String the remaining beads onto the pearl cotton #5 thread following the diagram at right. Refer to the guide on page 31 for knot instructions. Repeat steps 1 and 2 on page 31 to finish the end of the bracelet.

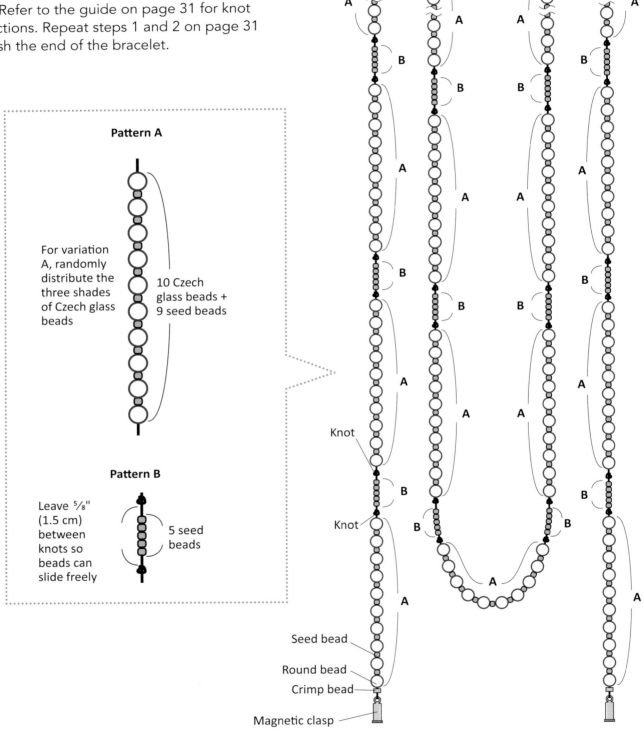

Pattern A

For variation A, randomly distribute the three shades of Czech glass beads

10 Czech glass beads + 9 seed beads

Pattern B

Leave ⅝" (1.5 cm) between knots so beads can slide freely

5 seed beads

Knot

Knot

Seed bead

Round bead

Crimp bead

Magnetic clasp

4. Attach one jump ring to the brass charm.

Jump ring

Brass charm

5. String the Swarovski crystal bead onto the head-pin. Cut the excess pin length and curl the tip into a loop. Attach one jump ring to the loop.

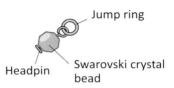

Jump ring

Headpin

Swarovski crystal bead

Refer to the Jewelry Making Technique Guide on pages 124-125 for detailed instructions on making headpin loops.

6. Link four jump rings together as shown in the diagram below.

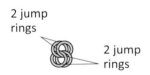

2 jump rings

2 jump rings

7. Attach the brass charm and the headpin charm to the set of jump rings. Attach the set of jump rings to the center of the bracelet

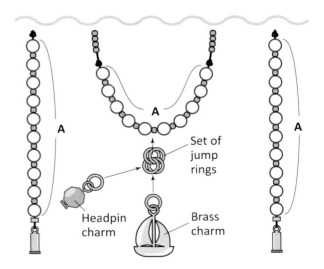

A

A

A

Set of jump rings

Headpin charm

Brass charm

Refer to the Jewelry Making Technique Guide on pages 124-125 for detailed instructions on attaching jump rings.

Sparkling Chiffon Bracelet & Necklace

Shown on page 20

FINISHED SIZE

▶ Bracelet: About 37 ½" (95 cm) long (should wrap around wrist 5 times)

▶ Necklace: About 41 ¼" (105 cm) long

MATERIALS

Bracelet

▶ 39 ½" (100 cm) of 3 mm wide rhinestone and silver cupchain

▶ Two rhodium 4 mm jump rings

▶ Two rhodium cupchain ends

▶ One rhodium toggle clasp

▶ 78 ¾" (200 cm) of 4 mm wide beige flat cord

▶ Two ¾" x 39 ½" (2 x 100 cm) strips of beige chiffon fabric

▶ Jewelry and beading glue

Necklace

▶ 19 ¾" (50 cm) of 3 mm wide rhinestone and silver cupchain

▶ 25 metallic gray 8 mm faceted round Czech glass beads

▶ 42 clear 6 mm faceted round Czech glass beads

▶ 110 silver 6 mm faceted round Czech glass beads

▶ 222 beige seed beads

▶ 25 antique silver 0.7 x 15 mm eyepins

▶ 42 brass 0.7 x 15 mm eyepins

▶ 10 rhodium 4 mm jump rings

▶ Two rhodium 10 mm twisted-finish jump rings

▶ Four antique silver medium-sized bead tips

▶ Two rhodium cupchain ends

▶ 39 ½" (100 cm) of 4 mm wide beige flat cord

▶ One ¾" x 39 ½" (2 x 100 cm) strip of beige chiffon fabric

▶ Two 78 ¾" (200 cm) long pieces of nylon beading thread

▶ Jewelry and beading glue

TOOLS

▶ Flat-nose pliers

▶ Round-nose pliers

▶ Wire cutters

INSTRUCTIONS

····················
Bracelet
····················

1. Insert one end of the cupchain into a cupchain end. Fold the side tabs over and squeeze to secure.

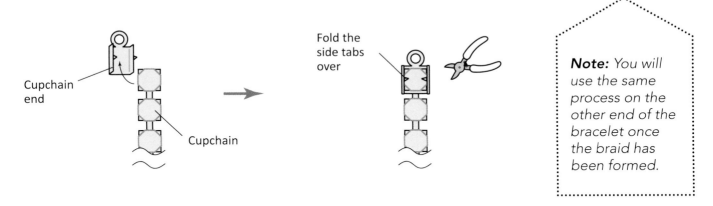

Cupchain end

Cupchain

Fold the side tabs over

Note: *You will use the same process on the other end of the bracelet once the braid has been formed.*

2. Tie the two chiffon strips to the cupchain and hide the knot. The chiffon will now be equal in length to the flat cord. Position the center of the flat cord underneath the cupchain. Form a three-strand braid using sections A, B, and C.

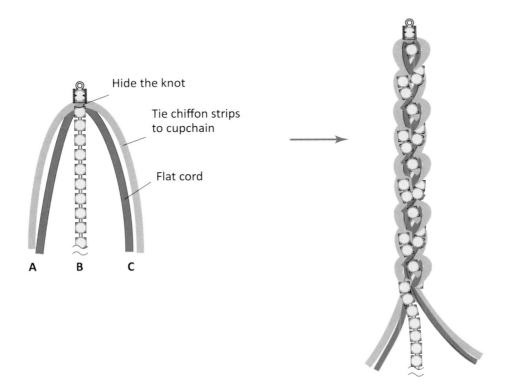

Hide the knot

Tie chiffon strips to cupchain

Flat cord

A   B   C

3. At the end of the braid, knot the chiffon and the flat cord behind the cupchain. Secure the ends with glue and hide the knot.

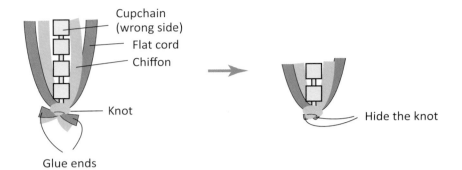

Cupchain (wrong side)

Flat cord

Chiffon

Knot

Glue ends

Hide the knot

4. Repeat step 1 on page 35 to attach the remaining cupchain end. Attach a jump ring and a toggle clasp component to each cupchain end.

Refer to the Jewelry Making Technique Guide on pages 124-125 for detailed instructions on attaching jump rings.

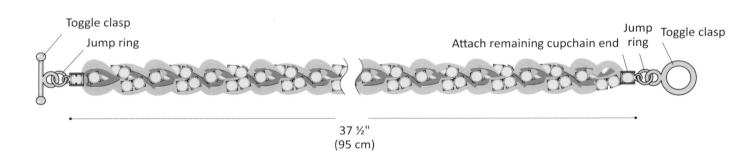

Toggle clasp

Jump ring

Attach remaining cupchain end

Jump ring

Toggle clasp

37 ½"
(95 cm)

Necklace

1. Make the braided section following the same process used to make the bracelet (see pages 35-36). Simply position the center of the chiffon strip under the cupchain rather than tying the strips as with the bracelet.

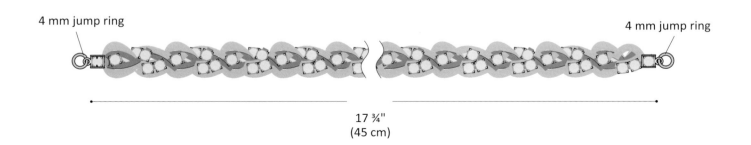

4 mm jump ring

4 mm jump ring

17 ¾"
(45 cm)

2. To make each Part A, string a bead onto an eyepin. Cut the excess pin length and curl the tip into a loop. Open and close the curled loops to connect 25 of Part A.

Refer to the Jewelry Making Technique Guide on pages 124-125 for detailed instructions on making eyepin loops.

Part A
(make 25)

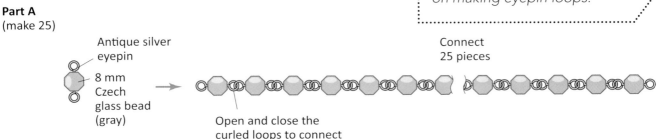

Antique silver eyepin

8 mm Czech glass bead (gray)

Open and close the curled loops to connect

Connect 25 pieces

3. To make each Part B, string a bead onto an eyepin. Cut the excess pin length and curl the tip into a loop. Open and close the curled loops to connect 42 of Part B.

Part B
(make 42)

Brass eyepin

6 mm Czech glass bead (clear)

Connect 42 pieces

4. String a bead tip onto a 78 ¾" (200 cm) long piece of nylon beading thread, then fold the thread in half. String the beads onto the doubled thread. Refer to the chart for bead quantities. String the remaining bead tip onto the thread and squeeze closed. Close the bead tip at the beginning in the same way.

Refer to the Jewelry Making Technique Guide on pages 124-125 for detailed instructions on using bead tips.

BEAD CHART

6 mm Czech glass beads	45
Seed beads	90

Part C

6 mm Czech glass bead (silver)

Bead tip   Seed beads

Bead tip

5. Follow the same process used to make Part C, but refer to the diagram below for bead pattern.

Part D

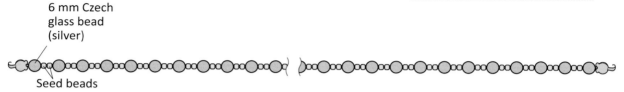

6 mm Czech glass bead (silver)

Seed beads

6. Attach a 4 mm jump ring to each end of Parts A-D. Attach each end of the braided section and each end of Parts A-D to the 10 mm twisted-finish jump rings.

Refer to the Jewelry Making Technique Guide on pages 124-125 for detailed instructions on attaching jump rings.

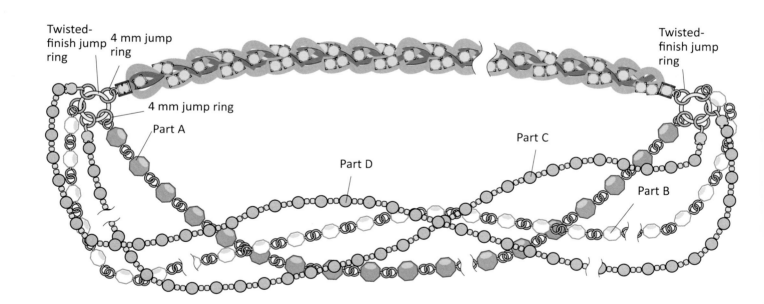

Twisted-finish jump ring

4 mm jump ring

4 mm jump ring

Part A

Part D

Part C

Part B

Twisted-finish jump ring

Simple Wrap Bracelets

Shown on page 22

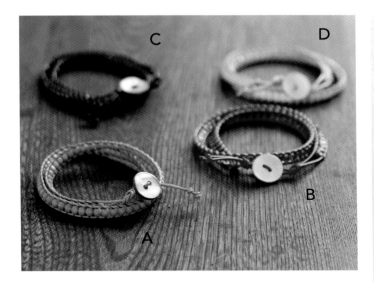

FINISHED SIZE

▸ About 15 ¾" (40 cm) long
(should wrap around the wrist twice)

MATERIALS

Refer to the Color Combination Chart for bead and cord colors for each bracelet variation.

▸ 85 4 mm Czech fire-polished glass beads
▸ 39 ½" (100 cm) of 1.2 mm round leather cord
▸ One ⅝" (15 mm) diameter mother-of-pearl button
▸ 137 ¾" (350 cm) of monofilament cord

COLOR COMBINATION CHART

	A	B	C	D
Czech glass beads	Turquoise	Clear purple	Hematite	Variegated white
Leather cord	Yellow	Hot pink	Purple	White
Mother-of-pearl button	Gray	Natural	Gray	Natural
Monofilament cord	Navy blue	Yellow	Red	Green

INSTRUCTIONS

Follow the same process used to make the Square Bead Wrap Bracelets, as shown in the Technique Overview on pages 23-25.

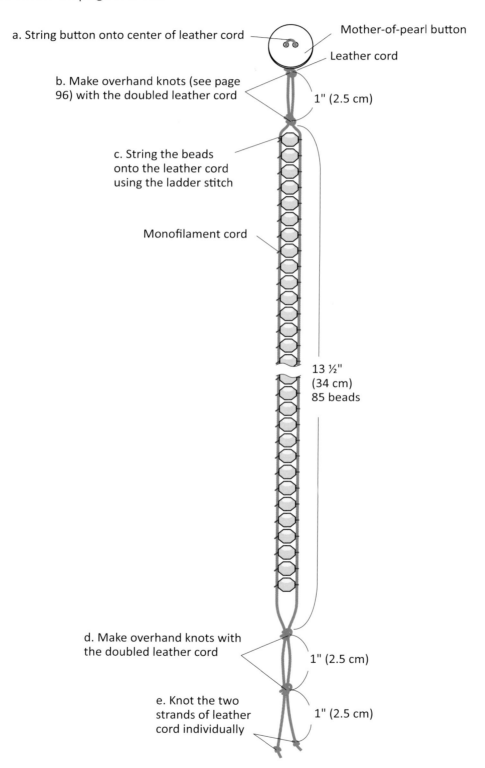

a. String button onto center of leather cord

Mother-of-pearl button

Leather cord

b. Make overhand knots (see page 96) with the doubled leather cord

1" (2.5 cm)

c. String the beads onto the leather cord using the ladder stitch

Monofilament cord

13 ½" (34 cm) 85 beads

d. Make overhand knots with the doubled leather cord

1" (2.5 cm)

e. Knot the two strands of leather cord individually

1" (2.5 cm)

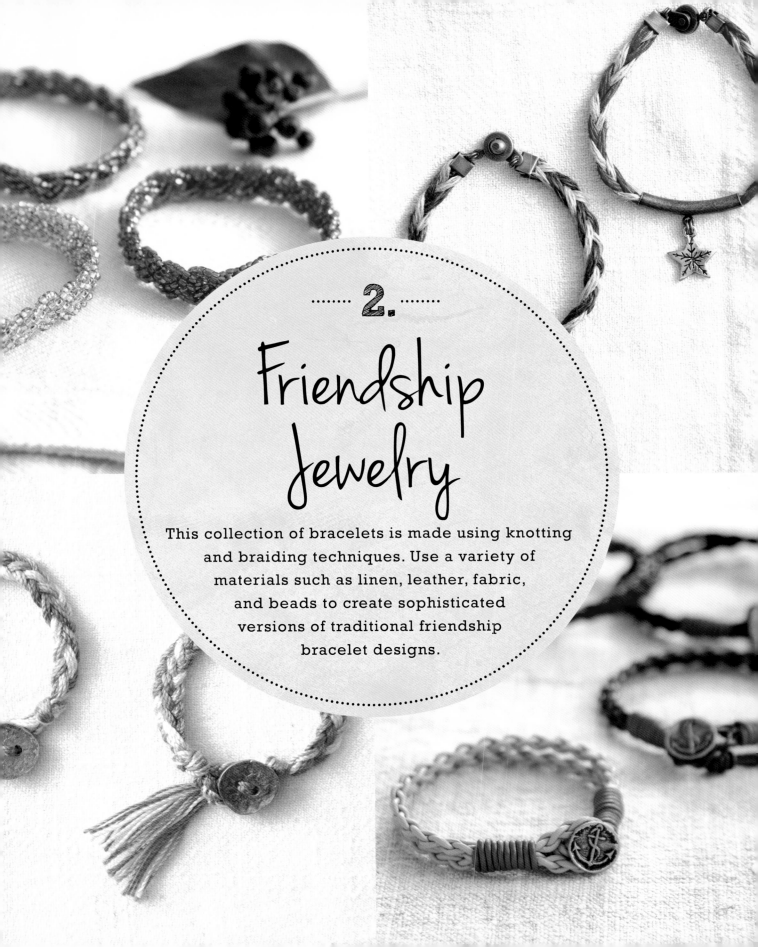

2.

Friendship Jewelry

This collection of bracelets is made using knotting and braiding techniques. Use a variety of materials such as linen, leather, fabric, and beads to create sophisticated versions of traditional friendship bracelet designs.

6 Linen Charm Bracelets

A

B

Braid linen cord, then add a metal charm for a simple and stylish bracelet. This design is perfect for layering with other styles.

Instructions on page 58

Braided Friendship Bracelets

Braid five different colors of embroidery floss to make this cheerful friendship bracelet. There are hundreds of colors of embroidery floss to choose from, so the possibilities are endless!

Instructions on page 50

A

B

Braided Seed Bead Bangle

String seed beads onto strands of wire, then braid to form this structured bracelet. Use bright, translucent seed beads as shown here for a tropical-inspired summertime look.

Instructions on page 61

Woven Fabric Bracelets

C

A

B

D

Put your leftover fabric scraps to work with this cheerful bracelet design. Simply cut your fabric into strips, braid, then attach a few charms. When selecting your fabric, look for small scale cotton prints, such as Liberty florals.

Instructions on page 63

Beaded Square Knot Bracelet

This bracelet features a flat rope of square knots embellished with metal beads. Experiment with different colors for the core and knotting cords for a two-tone effect. This design features an adjustable clasp made using a basic wrapped knot, so you can change the fit as desired.

Instructions on page 55

11 Square Knot Rope Amulets

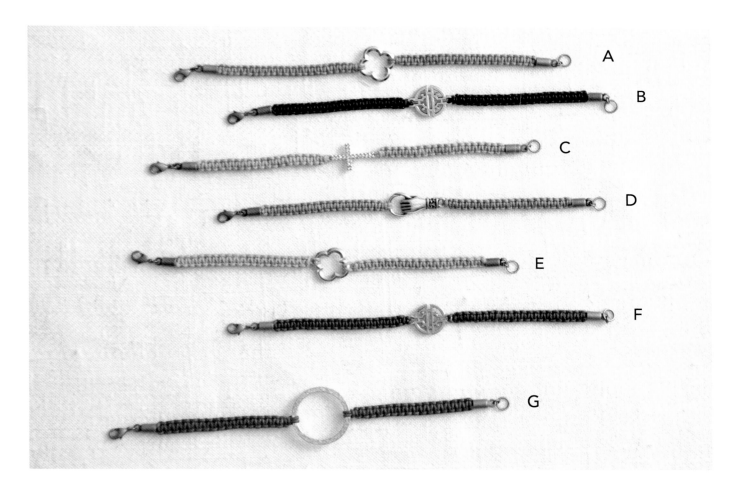

A

B

C

D

E

F

G

This bracelet is designed to showcase your favorite charm. Simply attach a piece of waxed cotton cord to each side of the charm, then form square knots. This bracelet is quick and easy to create, making it ideal for gift-giving.

Instructions on page 66

Doubled Rope Bracelet

This clean and simple bracelet design looks great on any wrist. Form a four-strand round braid, then fold the braid in half and secure with wrapped knots. Select a decorative button clasp as the focal point for the bracelet.

Instructions on page 53

Convertible Braid Bracelets

A

B

Also made using the four-strand round braid, this design can be worn as both a bracelet and a necklace. Make your own charms to add a decorative touch to this versatile piece.

Instructions on page 69

Friendship Jewelry Technique Overview

THE FIVE-STRAND BRAID

Just like a basic three-strand braid, this variation requires you to bring the outside cords to the center. The order may seem confusing at first, but once you start braiding, you'll have it memorized in no time.

The following guide uses Variation A as an example. Use the same technique for Variation B.

7 Braided Friendship Bracelets

Shown on page 43

A   B

MATERIALS

Refer to color combination chart for each bracelet variation.

▶ Two 29 ½" (75 cm) long pieces of DMC pearl cotton #5 embroidery thread in each color
▶ One ⅝" (15 mm) diameter button (with 3 mm diameter holes)

FINISHED SIZE

▶ About 8" (20 cm) long

COLOR COMBINATION CHART

A	B
Light pink (948)	Ivory (5)
Light blue (927)	Light blue (927)
Blue (807)	Blue (807)
Coral (351)	Gray (414)
Hot pink (3687)	Yellow (783)

INSTRUCTIONS

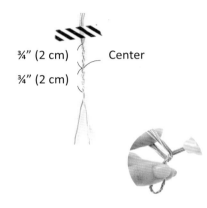

¾" (2 cm)   Center

¾" (2 cm)

1. Align all 10 pieces of thread (2 of each color). Divide the pieces into one group of 2 colors, one group of 1 color, and another group of 2 colors. Starting ¾" (2 cm) before the center, form a 1 ½" (4 cm) long three-strand braid. Fold the braid in half at the center and tie an overhand knot using all 10 pieces. This will be the button loop.

① ② ③ ④ ⑤

2. Tape the braided loop to your work surface. Group all four strands together for each color of thread. There will be five groups.

3. Bring ⑤ to position 2.

4. Bring ① to position 3.

5. Bring ② to position 3.

Make sure to pull the thread taut as you work. This will produce a flat and even braid.

6. Repeat steps 3-5 until the braid measures 4 ¾″ (12 cm) long. Note: You may need to adjust the length of the braid to fit your wrist size. Tie an overhand knot with all 10 pieces.

With the five-strand braid, you will repeatedly move the thread at position 5 to 2, position 1 to 3, and position 2 to 3. As you work, always keep the braid flat.

Overhand knot

7. String the button onto one color of thread. Tie an overhand knot with all 10 pieces to complete the bracelet.

THE FOUR-STRAND ROUND BRAID

This technique produces a nicely finished rope. When making this braid, always bring the outer cord toward the center. If you are unsure of which cord to bring to the center next, remember to use the "resting" cord.

The following guide uses the red leather variation as an example. Use the same technique for all colors.

Doubled Rope Bracelet

Shown on page 48

MATERIALS

▸ Two 49 ¼" (125 cm) long pieces of 1.5 mm round red, ivory, blue, or black leather cord

▸ Two 11 ¾" (30 cm) long pieces of 1.5 mm round taupe leather cord

▸ One ⅝" (15 mm) diameter shank button

FINISHED SIZE

▸ About 8" (20 cm) long

INSTRUCTIONS

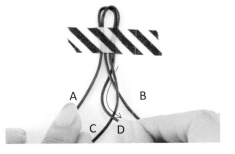

1. Fold the two 49 ¼" (125 cm) long pieces of cord in half at the center and tape to your work surface. Cross C over B.

2. Bring D under C and B. Cross D over C.

3. Bring A under D and C. Cross A over D.

4. Bring B under A and D. Cross B over A.

5. Bring C under A and B. Cross C over B. Repeat steps 2-5 until the braid measures 13 ½"-15" (34-38 cm), or double the size of your wrist.

6. Fold the braid in half. Make a basic wrapped knot using one of the 11 ¾" (30 cm) long pieces of round leather cord. To make the knot, form a loop starting about ¾" (2 cm) from the fold. Wrap the cord around the braid 10 times, then insert the cord end into the first loop and pull to tighten. Pull the other cord end to hide the loop under the wraps, then trim the excess.

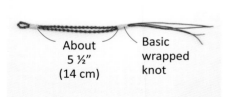  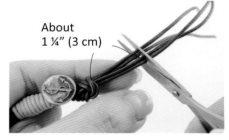

7. Make another basic wrapped knot about 5 ½" (14 cm) away from the knot made in step 6. Note: You may need to adjust the location of the knot to fit your wrist size. Cut the loops formed in step 1 and hide the cord ends under the basic wrapped knot.

8. String the button onto one strand of leather cord. Tie an overhand knot with all four strands.

9. Trim the cord ends 1 ¼" (3 cm) away from the knot to complete the bracelet.

THE SQUARE KNOT ROPE

Use this technique to create a flat rope of knots around core cords. Using two different colors of cord makes the knotting process easy and creates a fun design.

The following guide uses the navy and yellow variation as an example. Use the same technique for all colors.

Beaded Square Knot Bracelet

Shown on page 46

FINISHED SIZE

▸ About 8" (20 cm) long
  (this bracelet is adjustable)

MATERIALS

▸ Core cords: Two 15 ¾" (40 cm) long pieces of navy blue hemp cord
▸ Knotting cords: One 78 ¾" (200 cm) long piece of yellow, navy blue, or maroon hemp cord
▸ Bead A: One brass 6 x 8 mm tube-shaped spacer bead
▸ Bead B: Two brass 4 x 9 mm donut-shaped spacer beads
▸ Bead C: Two brass 3 x 6 mm donut-shaped spacer beads
▸ Jewelry and beading glue

TOOLS

▸ Crochet hook
▸ Toothpick

PROJECT DIAGRAM

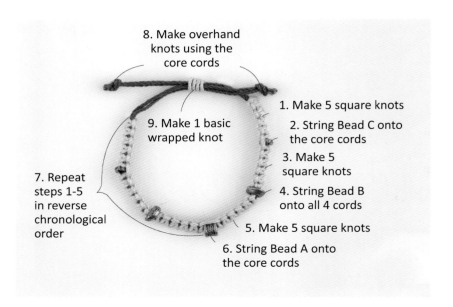

8. Make overhand knots using the core cords

1. Make 5 square knots

2. String Bead C onto the core cords

9. Make 1 basic wrapped knot

3. Make 5 square knots

4. String Bead B onto all 4 cords

7. Repeat steps 1-5 in reverse chronological order

5. Make 5 square knots

6. String Bead A onto the core cords

INSTRUCTIONS

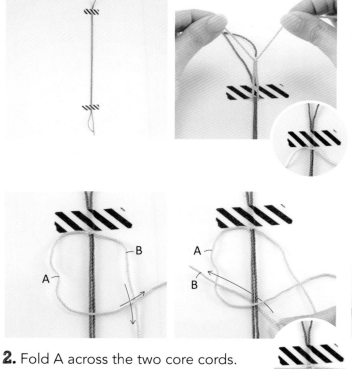

1. Align the two core cords, then tape them to your work surface at both the top and bottom. Tie the center of the knotting cord onto the core cords directly below the top piece of tape.

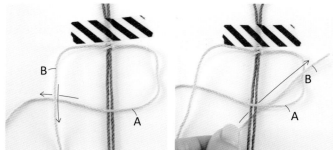

2. Fold A across the two core cords. Align B on top of A. Bring B under the core cords and through the loop made by A. Pull A and B to tighten.

3. Repeat step 2 folding A across the two core cords in the opposite direction. One square knot is now complete.

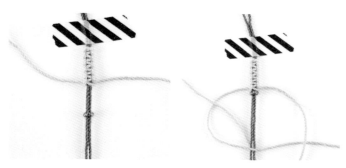

4. After making 5 square knots, string one Bead C onto the core cords. Make another 5 square knots.

5. String one Bead B onto all four cords (both core and knotting cords).

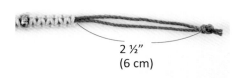

2 ½"
(6 cm)

6. Make 5 square knots. String Bead A onto the core cords. Continue knotting and stringing beads following step 7 in the Project Diagram on page 56. Use a crochet hook to weave the knotting cord ends under the final 2-3 knots. Trim the excess cord.

7. Using the core cords, make an overhand knot (see page 96) 2 ½" (6 cm) away from the final square knot. Trim the excess cord. Repeat at the other end of the bracelet.

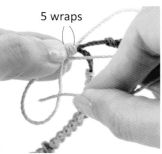

5 wraps

8. Overlap the core cords from each end of the bracelet. Use a scrap of cord to tie a basic wrapped knot (see step 6 on page 54).

9. Using a toothpick, apply dabs of glue to prevent the cords from unraveling. Trim the excess cord.

6 Linen Charm Bracelets

Shown on page 42

A

B

FINISHED SIZE

▸ About 6 ¼" (16 cm) long

MATERIALS

Refer to the Color Combination Chart for each bracelet variation.

▸ One brass 15 x 30 mm metal charm
▸ One brass 3.5 x 30 mm metal tube bead with loop
▸ Two brass 4.5 mm jump rings
▸ Four brass 3.5 mm jump rings
▸ One 19 ¾" (50 cm) long piece of linen cord in Color #1
▸ One 19 ¾" (50 cm) long piece of linen cord in Color #2
▸ Two brass cord ends
▸ One brass button clasp
▸ Tape

TOOLS

▸ Flat-nose pliers

COLOR COMBINATION CHART

	A	B
Metal charm	Cross	Star
Linen cord (Color #1)	Unbleached white	Unbleached white
Linen cord (Color #2)	Blue	Red

INSTRUCTIONS

1. Fold the two linen cords in half. String the brass tube bead onto the center of the two linen cords. There will now be four strands of cord on each side of the tube bead. Cut the looped cords at one end of the bracelet.

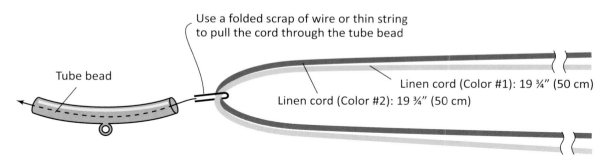

Use a folded scrap of wire or thin string to pull the cord through the tube bead

Tube bead

Linen cord (Color #1): 19 ¾" (50 cm)

Linen cord (Color #2): 19 ¾" (50 cm)

2. Form a three-strand variation braid on each side of the tube bead, as shown on page 60. Attach the cord ends to both ends of the bracelet.

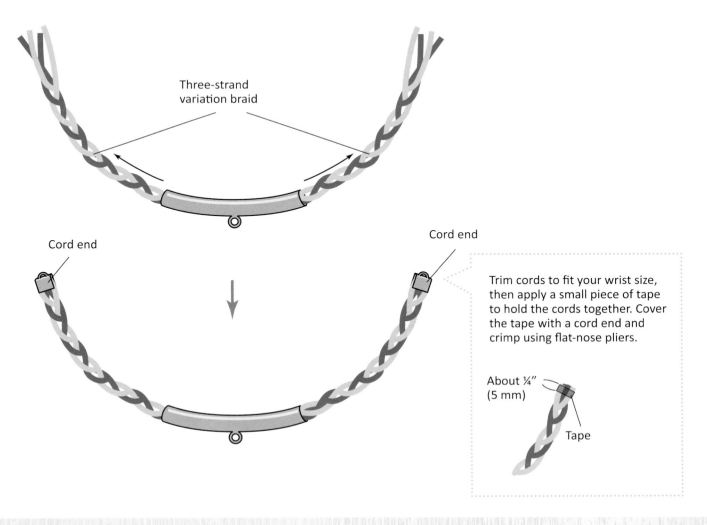

Three-strand variation braid

Cord end

Cord end

Trim cords to fit your wrist size, then apply a small piece of tape to hold the cords together. Cover the tape with a cord end and crimp using flat-nose pliers.

About ¼" (5 mm)

Tape

Three-Strand Variation Braid

 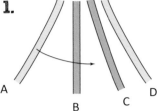

A B C D

 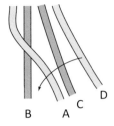

B A C D

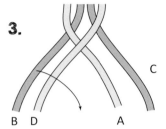

B D A C

4.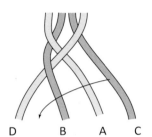

D B A C

5. Repeat steps 1 and 2.

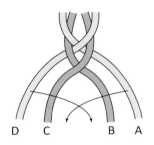

D C B A

6. The colors will alternate as you braid.

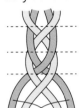 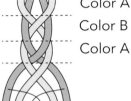

Color A
Color B
Color A

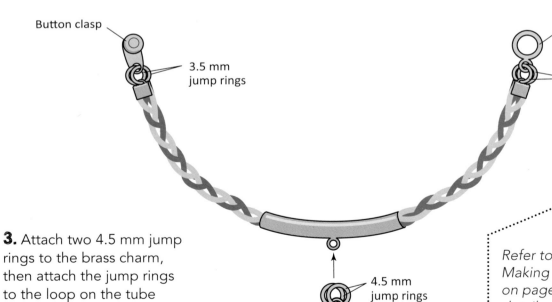

Button clasp

3.5 mm jump rings

Button clasp

3.5 mm jump rings

3. Attach two 4.5 mm jump rings to the brass charm, then attach the jump rings to the loop on the tube bead. Attach two 3.5 mm jump rings to each end of the bracelet. Attach the button clasp components to the jump rings.

4.5 mm jump rings

Brass charm

Refer to the Jewelry Making Technique Guide on pages 124-125 for detailed instructions on attaching jump rings.

Braided Seed Bead Bangle

Shown on page 44

FINISHED SIZE

▸ About 7" (18 cm) long

MATERIALS

▸ 810 yellow, purple, or turquoise 3-cut round size 11 seed beads
▸ One ⅜" (10 mm) diameter brown shank button
▸ 82 ½" (210 cm) of 22-gauge gold wire

TOOLS

▸ Wire cutters

INSTRUCTIONS

1. Cut the wire into three 27 ½" (70 cm) long pieces. String 17 ¾" (45 cm) of seed beads onto each piece of wire.

Make 3 strands

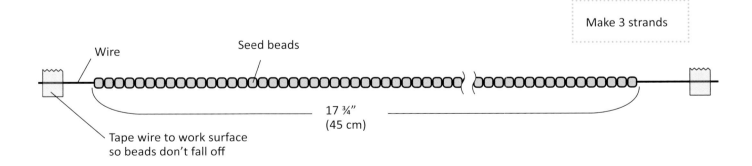

Wire

Seed beads

17 ¾"
(45 cm)

Tape wire to work surface so beads don't fall off

2. Align the three beaded strands. Twist the strands for 2"-2 ½" (5-6 cm) at the center, then fold in half to form a loop. Divide the strands into three groups of two. Form a three-strand braid for 5 ¾" (14.5 cm).

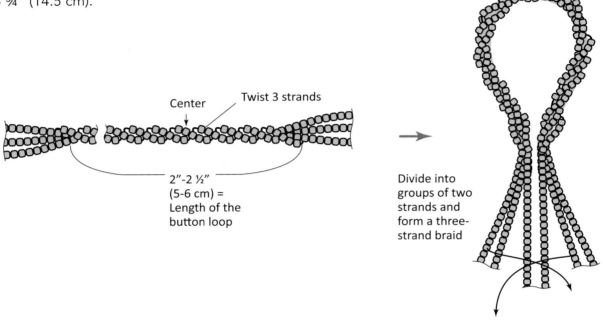

Center

Center

Twist 3 strands

2"-2 ½" (5-6 cm) = Length of the button loop

Divide into groups of two strands and form a three-strand braid

3. String the button onto all six strands of wire. Form the wire ends into a loop. Coil a couple of strands of wire around the others, then trim the excess.

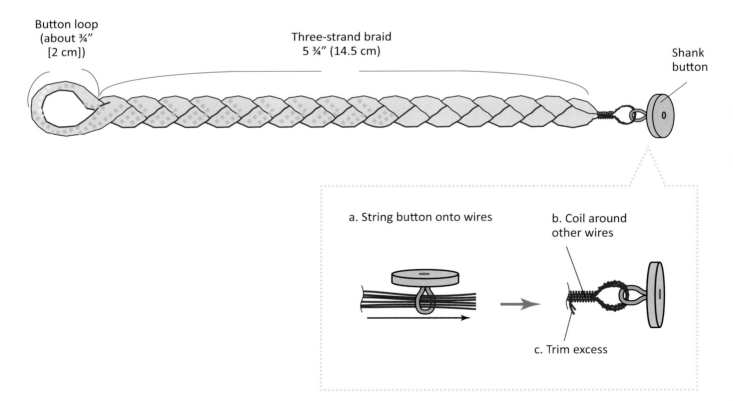

Button loop (about ¾" [2 cm])

Three-strand braid 5 ¾" (14.5 cm)

Shank button

a. String button onto wires

b. Coil around other wires

c. Trim excess

Woven Fabric Bracelets

Shown on page 45

A

C

B

D

FINISHED SIZE

▸ About 15 ¾" (40 cm) long (should wrap around the wrist twice)

MATERIALS

Refer to the Color Combination Chart for each bracelet variation.

▸ Two oval metal beads
▸ Two metal charms
▸ Nine rhodium 6 mm twisted-finish jump rings
▸ Eight antique silver 4 mm jump rings
▸ Two rhodium 0.6 x 30 mm headpins
▸ One ⅝" (15 mm) diameter oval shank button
▸ One 2 ½" x 21 ¼" (6 x 54 cm) piece of cotton fabric

TOOLS

▸ Flat-nose pliers
▸ Round-nose pliers
▸ Wire cutters

COLOR COMBINATION CHART

	A	B	C	D
Oval metal beads	Silver	Silver	Silver	Silver
Charms	Antique silver leaf	Antique silver elephant	Antique silver lion	Antique silver bear
Cotton fabric	Green print	Light blue print	Pink print	Blue print
Button	Brown	Unbleached white	Light brown	Black

INSTRUCTIONS

1. Cut the fabric into three ¾" x 21 ¼" (2 x 54 cm) strips. For each strip, fold each long edge in ¼" (5 mm) and press, then fold in half and press again.

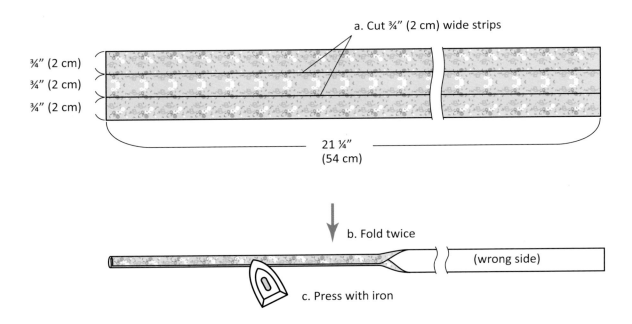

a. Cut ¾" (2 cm) wide strips

¾" (2 cm)
¾" (2 cm)
¾" (2 cm)

21 ¼"
(54 cm)

b. Fold twice

(wrong side)

c. Press with iron

2. Using the three folded strips, form a 15 ¾" (40 cm) long three-strand braid. String the button onto one strip. Use one strip to tie a slip knot around the other two. Trim the strip ends on the diagonal.

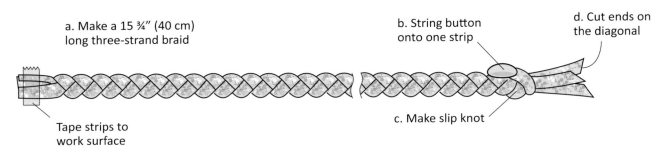

a. Make a 15 ¾" (40 cm) long three-strand braid

Tape strips to work surface

b. String button onto one strip

d. Cut ends on the diagonal

c. Make slip knot

3. String an oval bead onto a headpin. Cut the excess pin length and curl the tip into a loop. Attach one 4 mm jump ring to the loop, then attach another 4 mm jump ring to the first one. Repeat process to make another oval bead charm.

4. Attach one 4 mm jump ring to one of the silver charms. Attach another 4 mm jump ring to the first one. Repeat process to make another charm.

Two 4 mm jump rings

Oval bead

Headpin

Two 4 mm jump rings

Silver charm

Refer to the Jewelry Making Technique Guide on pages 124-125 for detailed instructions on making headpin loops and attaching jump rings.

5. Form the unfinished end of the bracelet into a loop. Secure the loop in place using one of the 6 mm jump rings and flat-nose pliers. Attach two 6 mm jump rings every 2 ¾" (7 cm). Attach the four charms to each set of jump rings.

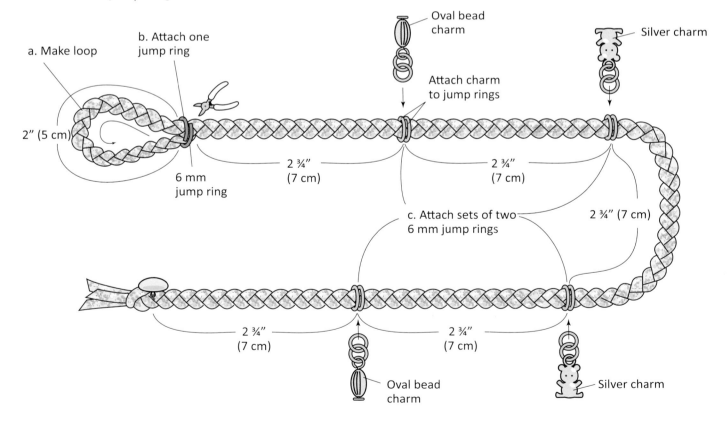

Oval bead charm

Silver charm

a. Make loop

b. Attach one jump ring

Attach charm to jump rings

2" (5 cm)

6 mm jump ring

2 ¾" (7 cm)

2 ¾" (7 cm)

c. Attach sets of two 6 mm jump rings

2 ¾" (7 cm)

2 ¾" (7 cm)

2 ¾" (7 cm)

Oval bead charm

Silver charm

Square Knot Rope Amulets

Shown on page 47

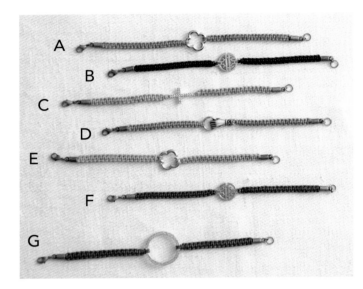

FINISHED SIZE

▸ About 6" (15 cm) long

MATERIALS

Refer to the Color Combination Chart for each bracelet variation.

▸ One metal decorative connector
▸ Two 3.5 mm jump rings
▸ One 6 mm jump ring
▸ Two 3 mm diameter cord ends
▸ One lobster clasp
▸ 102 ¼" (260 cm) of 0.5 mm wide waxed cotton cord
▸ Jewelry and beading glue

TOOLS

▸ Flat-nose pliers
▸ Toothpick

COLOR COMBINATION CHART

		A	B	C	D	E	F	G
Metal decorative connector	Shape	Flower-shaped ring	Round cut-out design	Cross	Hand holding a ring	Flower-shaped ring	Round cut-out design	Ring
	Color	Rhodium	Brass	Rhodium	Brass	Gold	Rhodium	Rhodium
	Size	15 mm diameter	13 mm diameter	11 x 18 mm	10 x 25 mm	15 mm diameter	13 mm diameter	25 mm diameter
Findings		Antique silver	Brass	Antique silver	Brass	Brass	Antique silver	Antique silver
Waxed cotton cord		Light blue	Black	Green	Light brown	Orange	Brown	Blue

INSTRUCTIONS

1. Cut two 15 ¾" (40 cm) long pieces of waxed cotton cord. Fold each piece in half and tie to one side of the decorative connector as shown in the diagram below.

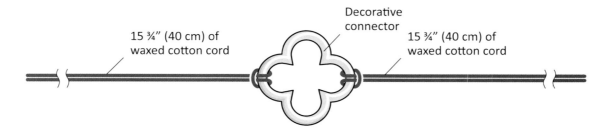

Decorative connector

15 ¾" (40 cm) of waxed cotton cord

15 ¾" (40 cm) of waxed cotton cord

2. Cut two 35 ½" (90 cm) long pieces of waxed cotton cord. Make a square knot rope on each side of the charm (see page 56). Refer to the diagram below for square knot rope length.

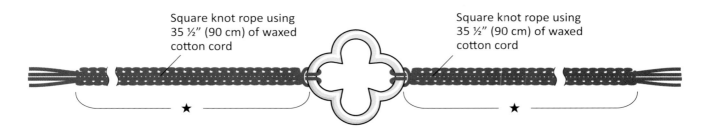

Square knot rope using 35 ½" (90 cm) of waxed cotton cord

Square knot rope using 35 ½" (90 cm) of waxed cotton cord

★ = Square knot rope length
A, B, E, and F = 2 ½" (6 cm)
C and D = 2 ¼" (5.5 cm)
G = 2" (5 cm)

3. Attach a cord end to each end of the bracelet, then attach a 3.5 mm jump ring to each cord end. Attach the lobster clasp to one 3.5 mm jump ring and the 6 mm jump ring to the other.

Refer to the Technique Overview on pages 124-125 for detailed instructions on attaching jump rings.

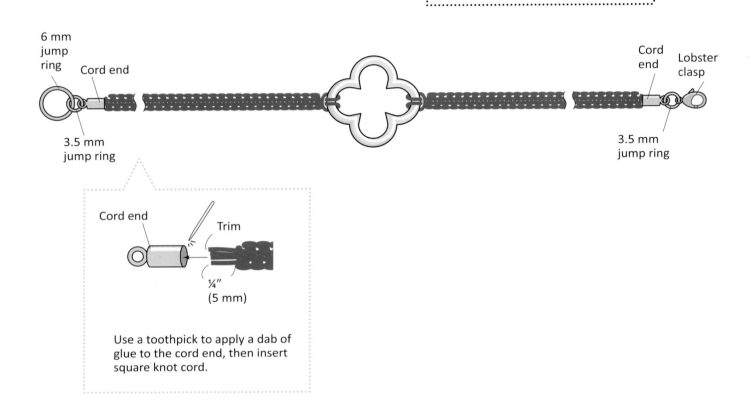

6 mm jump ring

Cord end

3.5 mm jump ring

Cord end

Lobster clasp

3.5 mm jump ring

Cord end

Trim

¼" (5 mm)

Use a toothpick to apply a dab of glue to the cord end, then insert square knot cord.

13 Convertible Braid Bracelets

Shown on page 49

FINISHED SIZE

▸ About 33 ½" (85 cm) long

COLOR COMBINATION CHART

	A	B
Natural stone bead	Turquoise	Red tiger eye
Leather cord	Navy blue	Black

MATERIALS

Refer to the Color Combination Chart for each bracelet variation.

▸ One antique silver ½" (13 mm) diameter shank button
▸ One ½" (13 mm) black onyx cross bead
▸ One 5 mm diameter natural stone bead
▸ One antique silver 5 mm donut-shaped spacer bead
▸ Three rhodium 4.5 mm jump rings
▸ Two rhodium 0.7 x 35 mm headpins
▸ 196 ¾" (500 cm) of 1.5 mm round leather cord

TOOLS

▸ Round-nose pliers
▸ Flat-nose pliers
▸ Wire cutters

INSTRUCTIONS

1. Cut the leather cord into two pieces. Fold one piece in half, forming a 2" (5 cm) loop. Fold the other piece in half and tie to the first piece of cord in order to secure the loop in place. Form a 31 ½" (80 cm) long four-strand round braid (see page 53).

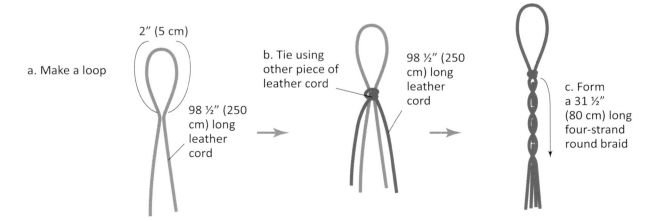

a. Make a loop — 2" (5 cm) — 98 ½" (250 cm) long leather cord

b. Tie using other piece of leather cord — 98 ½" (250 cm) long leather cord

c. Form a 31 ½" (80 cm) long four-strand round braid

2. Use one strand of leather cord to tie a slip knot around the other three (see page 96). String the button onto one strand, then tie another slip knot using one strand. Trim the excess cord. Make the headpin charms and attach them to the first slip knot using the jump rings.

Refer to the Jewelry Making Technique Guide on pages 124-125 for detailed instructions on making headpin loops and attaching jump rings.

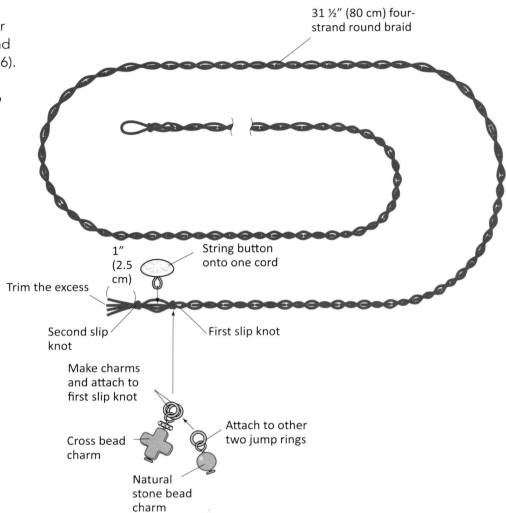

31 ½" (80 cm) four-strand round braid

String button onto one cord

1" (2.5 cm)

Trim the excess

Second slip knot

First slip knot

Make charms and attach to first slip knot

Attach to other two jump rings

Cross bead charm

Natural stone bead charm

How to Make the Charms

2 jump rings

Metal spacer bead

Cross bead

String the cross and metal spacer bead onto a headpin. Cut the excess pin length and curl the tip of the pin into a loop. Attach two jump rings to the loop.

Natural stone bead

Jump ring

Headpin

String the natural stone bead onto a headpin. Cut the excess pin length and curl the tip of the pin into a loop. Attach one jump ring to the loop.

3.

Classic Jewelry

This collection features elegant styles made with natural gemstones and pearls. Whenever possible, opt for high quality materials such as gold-plated clasps and detailed buttons. Using well-made components will allow you to enjoy these classic styles for years to come.

Turquoise Bracelets

Showcase the natural beauty of turquoise with these simple bracelet designs. Variation A uses heishi beads, a term used for small tube-shaped beads made of shell or stone. Variation B features large, statement-making turquoise stones embellished with a metal charm.

Instructions on page 84

A

B

Wire Work Bracelets

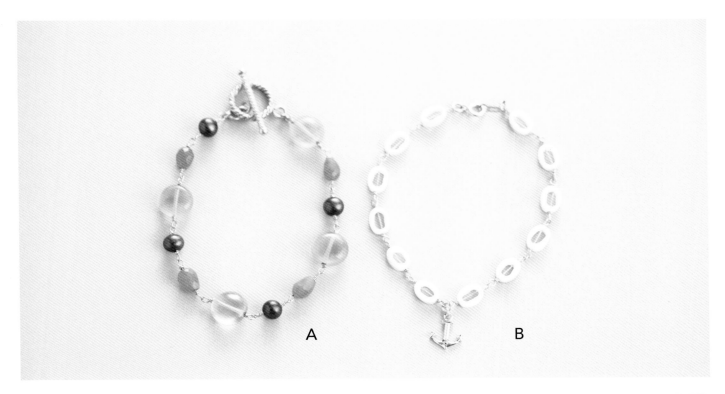

A   B

Create wrapped wire loops to connect natural gemstone beads for these feminine bracelets. Variation A features a combination of yellow fluorite, red aventurine, and brown freshwater pearls, while Variation B is made with mother-of-pearl shell beads.

Instructions on page 80

Combine several natural gemstone bracelets for an organically layered look.

Cotton Pearl Bracelets & Long Necklace

String pearls and a rhinestone button onto thread to create this elegant bracelet and necklace set. These designs feature cotton pearls, which are surprisingly lightweight and more affordable than genuine pearls.

Instructions on page 87

For a completely different look, wrap the necklace around your wrist multiple times for a statement-making bracelet.

Champagne Pearl Set

This complex-looking bracelet is deceptively simple to make. Just string the beads onto colored thread and alternate with overhand knots. Complete the set with the matching earrings and ring made with decorative headpin loops.

Instructions on page 91

For a different look, try using a pink color scheme, as shown here.

18 Beaded Brooch Bracelet

These beaded brooches look good enough to eat! Sew similarly colored beads onto geometric felt cutouts. Wear as a brooch or string onto a piece of black ribbon to transform the design into a bracelet.

Instructions on page 97

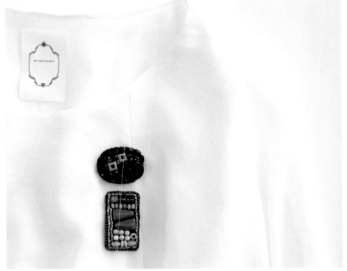

Pin the brooch to a simple blouse to add a dose of glamor to any outfit.

Classic Jewelry Technique Overview

THE WRAPPED LOOP

With this method, you'll form wire loops that can be used to connect beads. Twisting the wire into loops creates a strong connection, so this technique is ideal for projects that use larger, heavier beads.

Wire Work Bracelets

Shown on page 73

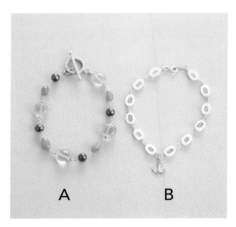

A   B

FINISHED SIZE

- Orange Bracelet (A): About 7 ½" (19 cm) long
- White Bracelet (B): 7" (18 cm) long

MATERIALS

Orange Bracelet (A)

- Four 10 mm yellow fluorite beads
- Four brown 6 mm freshwater pearls
- Four 6 x 8 mm teardrop-shaped red aventurine beads
- One 13 mm 24K gold-plated toggle clasp
- Four 4 mm 14K gold-plated jump rings
- 39 ½" (100 cm) of 26-gauge gold wire

White Bracelet (B)

- 12 white 8 mm oval cutout shell beads
- One 9 x 11 mm 18K gold-plated anchor charm
- Four 4 mm 14K gold-plated jump rings
- One 5 mm 14K gold-plated spring clasp with tab
- 39 ½" (100 cm) of 26-gauge gold wire

TOOLS

- Round-nose pliers
- Flat-nose pliers
- Wire cutters

BEAD PATTERNS

Orange Bracelet (A)

Jump ring

Toggle clasp

Jump rings

Toggle clasp

White Bracelet (B)

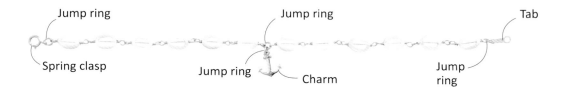

Jump ring

Spring clasp

Jump ring

Jump ring

Charm

Tab

Jump ring

INSTRUCTIONS

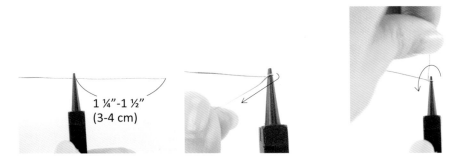

1 ¼"-1 ½"
(3-4 cm)

1. Using round-nose pliers, pinch the 39 ½" (100 cm) long piece of wire about 1 ¼"-1 ½" (3-4 cm) from the right end. Curl the end of the wire around the tip of the pliers. Use your fingers to wrap the end around the long section of wire two times. Position the wraps flush against the tip of the pliers.

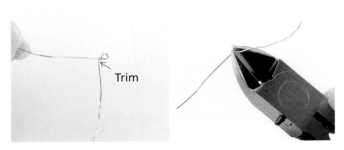

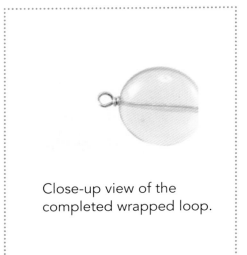

2. Remove the pliers. The wrapped loop is complete. Trim the short wire end close to the loop.

Close-up view of the completed wrapped loop.

3. String the first bead onto the wire following the bead pattern on page 81. Using round-nose pliers, pinch the wire 1 mm from the bead. Make a wrapped loop, then trim the excess wire.

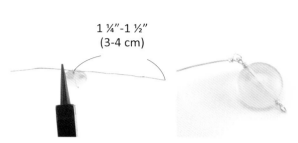

1 ¼"-1 ½"
(3-4 cm)

Jump
ring

Jump
ring

4. Insert the wire through one of the wrapped loops for 1 ¼"-1 ½" (3-4 cm). Make a wrapped loop and trim the excess wire. Following the bead pattern on page 81, continue connecting beads using wrapped loops.

For White Bracelet (B)
Use wrapped loops to attach a jump ring at the center of the bracelet (see step 5 below). Attach another jump ring to the charm, then connect the two jump rings.

Tab

Spring
clasp

5. Once all the beads have been connected, you will use jump rings to attach clasp components to both ends of the bracelet. Using pliers, open each jump ring vertically. Attach a jump ring to each clasp component, then close the jump rings vertically.

For White Bracelet (B)
Follow the same process to attach jump rings to the spring clasp and tab.

14 Turquoise Bracelets

Shown on page 72

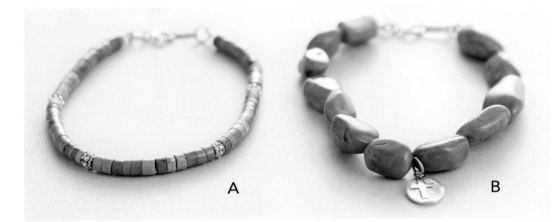

A

B

FINISHED SIZE

▶ About 6 ¾" (17 cm) long

INSTRUCTIONS

Heishi Bead Bracelet (A)

1. String a couple of heishi beads, a crimp bead, and the wire coil onto the cord to start the bracelet.

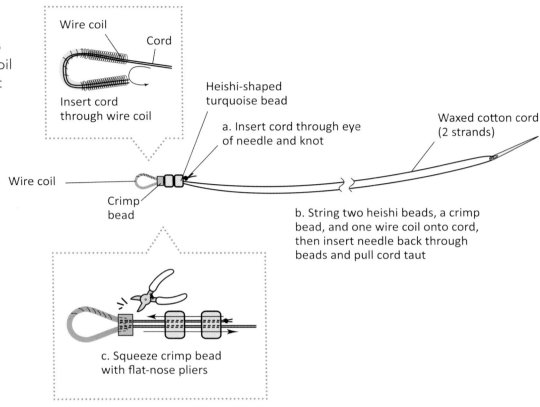

Wire coil

Cord

Insert cord through wire coil

Heishi-shaped turquoise bead

a. Insert cord through eye of needle and knot

Waxed cotton cord (2 strands)

Wire coil

Crimp bead

b. String two heishi beads, a crimp bead, and one wire coil onto cord, then insert needle back through beads and pull cord taut

c. Squeeze crimp bead with flat-nose pliers

2. String the remaining beads onto the cord following the pattern shown in the diagram below. Follow the same process used in step 1 to attach the other crimp bead and wire coil. Attach a jump ring to each end of the bracelet. Attach the spring clasp to one of the jump rings and the tab to the other.

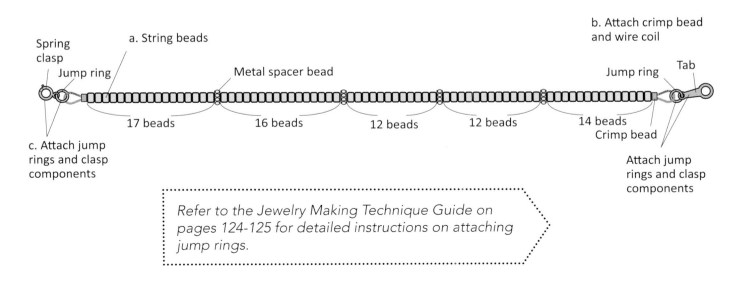

b. Attach crimp bead and wire coil

Spring clasp

Jump ring

a. String beads

Metal spacer bead

Jump ring

Tab

c. Attach jump rings and clasp components

17 beads

16 beads

12 beads

12 beads

14 beads

Crimp bead

Attach jump rings and clasp components

Refer to the Jewelry Making Technique Guide on pages 124-125 for detailed instructions on attaching jump rings.

Nugget Bead Bracelet (B)

Follow the same process used to make the Heishi Bead Bracelet (see page 85), but refer to the diagram below for bead pattern. Attach the remaining jump ring to the metal charm, then attach the jump ring to the center of the bracelet.

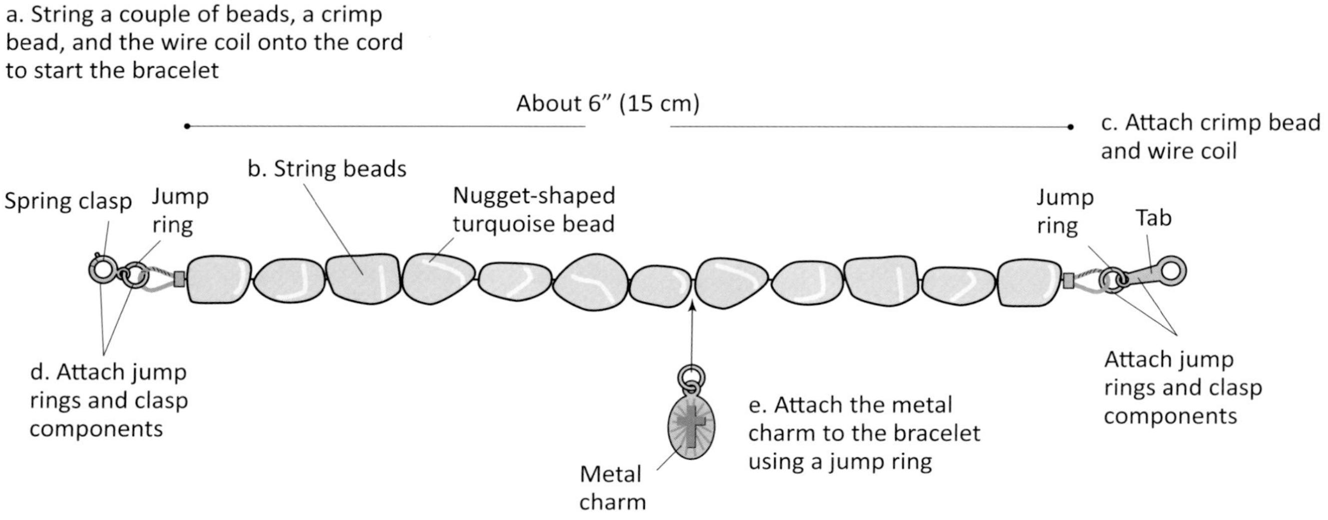

a. String a couple of beads, a crimp bead, and the wire coil onto the cord to start the bracelet

About 6" (15 cm)

c. Attach crimp bead and wire coil

Spring clasp   Jump ring

b. String beads

Nugget-shaped turquoise bead

Jump ring   Tab

d. Attach jump rings and clasp components

Attach jump rings and clasp components

Metal charm

e. Attach the metal charm to the bracelet using a jump ring

Refer to the Jewelry Making Technique Guide on pages 124-125 for detailed instructions on attaching jump rings.

Cotton Pearl Bracelets & Long Necklace

Shown on page 74

FINISHED SIZE

- Bracelets: About 7" (18 cm) long
- Necklace: About 53 ¼" (135 cm) long

MATERIALS

Gray Bracelet

- Nine gray 10 mm round cotton pearls
- Nine gray 8 mm round cotton pearls
- Two gray 3 mm round keshi pearls
- One ⅜" (10 mm) square rhinestone button
- One bronze crimp bead
- 2" (5 cm) of bronze chain
- 31 ½" (80 cm) of beading thread

White Bracelet

- Nine white 10 mm round cotton pearls
- Nine white 8 mm round cotton pearls
- Two white 3 mm round keshi pearls
- One ½" (12 mm) cone-shaped rhinestone button
- One bronze crimp bead
- 2" (5 cm) of bronze chain
- 31 ½" (80 cm) of beading thread

Necklace

- 15 white 10 mm round cotton pearls
- 15 gray 10 mm round cotton pearls
- 30 white 8 mm round cotton pearls
- 30 gray 8 mm round cotton pearls
- 182 white 3 mm round keshi pearls
- One 1" (24 mm) round rhinestone button
- One bronze crimp bead
- 2 ½" (6 cm) of bronze chain
- 118 ¼" (300 cm) of beading thread

TOOLS

- Beading needle
- Flat-nose pliers

INSTRUCTIONS

Gray Bracelet

1. String the rhinestone button onto the thread.

b. Insert thread through eye of needle

a. Position button at center of thread

Beading needle

Rhinestone button

2. String the beads onto the thread.

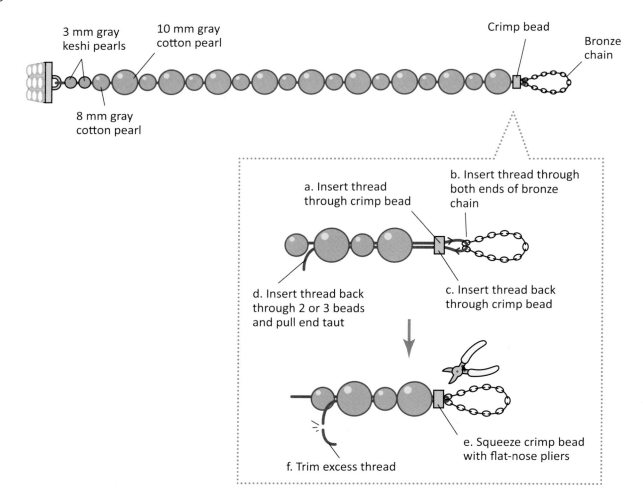

3 mm gray keshi pearls

10 mm gray cotton pearl

Crimp bead

Bronze chain

8 mm gray cotton pearl

a. Insert thread through crimp bead

b. Insert thread through both ends of bronze chain

d. Insert thread back through 2 or 3 beads and pull end taut

c. Insert thread back through crimp bead

e. Squeeze crimp bead with flat-nose pliers

f. Trim excess thread

White Bracelet

1. String the rhinestone button onto the thread.

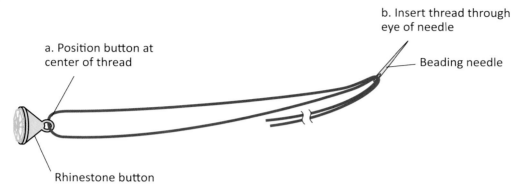

b. Insert thread through eye of needle

a. Position button at center of thread

Beading needle

Rhinestone button

2. String the beads onto the thread.

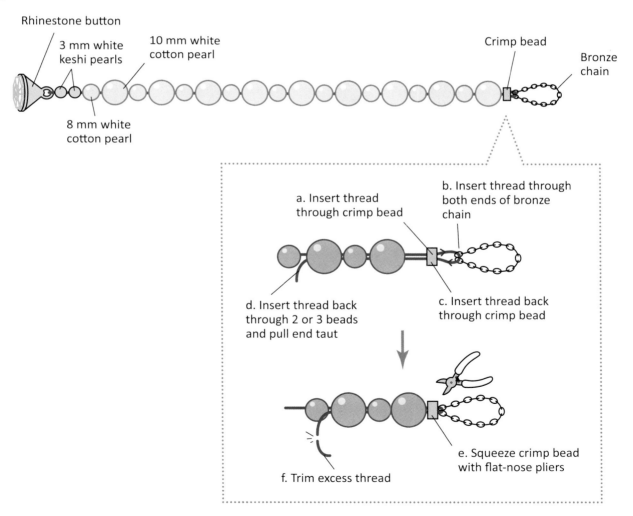

Rhinestone button

3 mm white keshi pearls

10 mm white cotton pearl

Crimp bead

Bronze chain

8 mm white cotton pearl

a. Insert thread through crimp bead

b. Insert thread through both ends of bronze chain

d. Insert thread back through 2 or 3 beads and pull end taut

c. Insert thread back through crimp bead

e. Squeeze crimp bead with flat-nose pliers

f. Trim excess thread

Necklace

Follow the same process used to make the Gray Bracelet (see page 88), but refer to the diagram below for bead pattern.

Repeat ★ pattern a total of 15 times

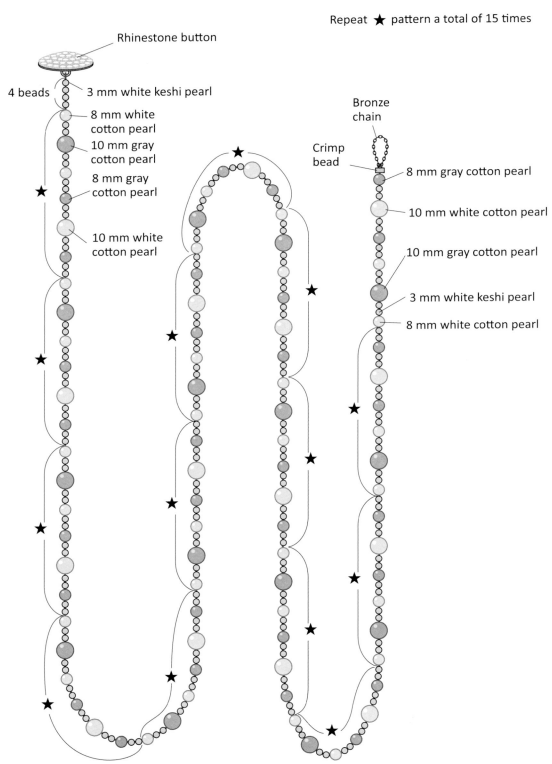

Rhinestone button

4 beads

3 mm white keshi pearl

8 mm white cotton pearl

10 mm gray cotton pearl

8 mm gray cotton pearl

10 mm white cotton pearl

Bronze chain

Crimp bead

8 mm gray cotton pearl

10 mm white cotton pearl

10 mm gray cotton pearl

3 mm white keshi pearl

8 mm white cotton pearl

Champagne Pearl Set

Shown on page 76

FINISHED SIZE

▸ Bracelets: About 8 ¼"
   (21 cm) long

▸ Earrings: About 2 ¼"
   (5.5 cm) high

▸ Ring: About 1 ½"
   (3.5 cm) high

MATERIALS

Turquoise Bracelet

▸ 24 champagne gold 8 mm
   round cotton pearls

▸ Eight turquoise 6 mm round
   Swarovski crystal pearls

▸ Eight brass 7 mm
   barrel-shaped spacer beads

▸ One brass ⅝" (16 mm)
   diameter button

▸ 315" (800 cm) of teal Amiet
   beading thread

Pink Bracelet

▸ 24 champagne gold 8 mm
   round cotton pearls

▸ Eight pink coral 6 mm round
   Swarovski crystal pearls

▸ Eight brass 7 mm
   barrel-shaped spacer beads

▸ One brass ⅝" (16 mm)
   diameter button

▸ 315" (800 cm) of mahogany
   Amiet beading thread

Earrings

▸ Two white 10 mm round
   cotton pearls

▸ Six champagne gold 8 mm
   round cotton pearls

▸ Four turquoise 6 mm round
   Swarovski crystal pearls

▸ 10 brass 7 mm barrel-shaped
   spacer beads

▸ Four gold 0.5 x 20 mm ball
   headpins

▸ Six gold 0.6 x 30 mm ball
   headpins

▸ One set of gold 1 ½" (4 cm)
   diameter hoop earring bases

Ring

▸ One white 10 mm round
   cotton pearl

▸ One pink coral 6 mm round
   Swarovski crystal pearl

▸ One brass 7 mm barrel-shaped
   metal spacer bead

▸ One gold 0.5 x 20 mm ball
   headpin

▸ Two gold 0.6 x 30 mm ball
   headpins

▸ One textured gold ring base
   with loop

TOOLS

Bracelets

▸ Beading needle

Earrings & Ring

▸ Round-nose pliers

▸ Flat-nose pliers

▸ Wire cutters

INSTRUCTIONS

....
Bracelets
....

1. Cut the beading thread into eight 39 ½" (100 cm) long pieces. Divide the thread into one group of three pieces, one group of two pieces, and another group of three pieces. Starting 1 ¼" (3 cm) before the center, form a 2 ½" (6 cm) long three-strand braid.

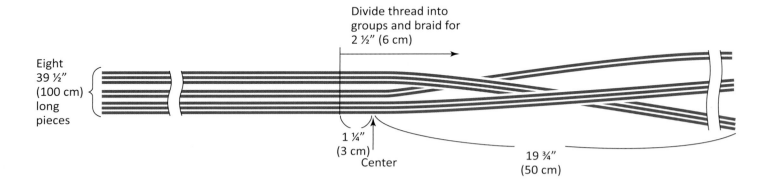

Divide thread into groups and braid for 2 ½" (6 cm)

Eight 39 ½" (100 cm) long pieces

1 ¼" (3 cm)
Center

19 ¾" (50 cm)

2. Tie an overhand knot (see page 96) to form the braid into a button loop. Using a beading needle, thread a cotton pearl onto two strands of thread.

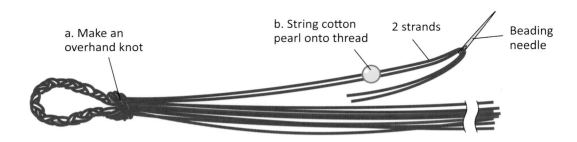

a. Make an overhand knot

b. String cotton pearl onto thread

2 strands

Beading needle

3. Join two strands of thread together with the two beaded strands and tie an overhand knot. Continue beading and knotting following the diagram below. This will create four beaded rows of four strands each.

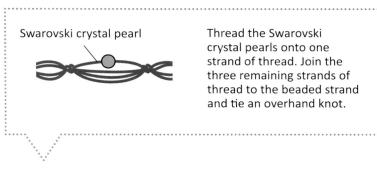

Swarovski crystal pearl

Thread the Swarovski crystal pearls onto one strand of thread. Join the three remaining strands of thread to the beaded strand and tie an overhand knot.

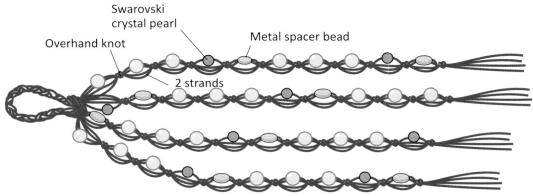

Overhand knot

Swarovski crystal pearl

Metal spacer bead

2 strands

4. Join the four beaded rows together. Use one beaded row to tie a slip knot around the other three (see page 96). String the button onto four strands, then tie an overhand knot using all 16 strands. Trim the excess thread.

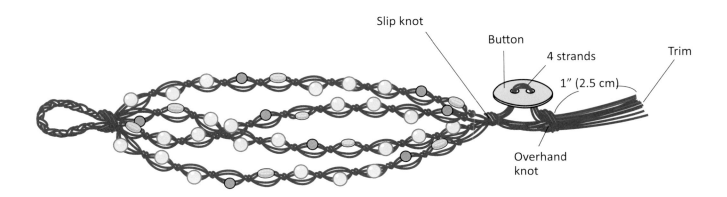

Slip knot

Button

4 strands

Trim

1" (2.5 cm)

Overhand knot

Earrings

1. For each part, string the beads onto the head-pins. Cut the excess pin length and curl the tips into loops.

Refer to the Jewelry Making Technique Guide on pages 124-125 for detailed instructions on making headpin loops.

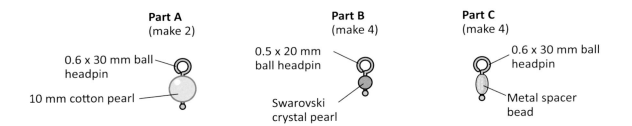

Part A
(make 2)

0.6 x 30 mm ball headpin

10 mm cotton pearl

Part B
(make 4)

0.5 x 20 mm ball headpin

Swarovski crystal pearl

Part C
(make 4)

0.6 x 30 mm ball headpin

Metal spacer bead

2. String the remaining beads and the headpin loops onto the earring bases following the diagram below

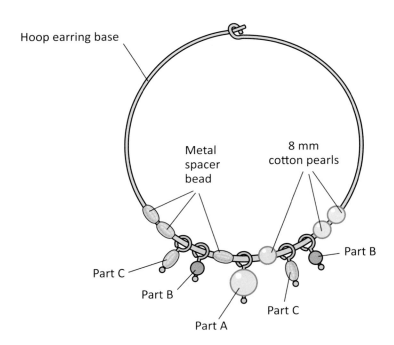

Hoop earring base

Metal spacer bead

8 mm cotton pearls

Part B

Part C

Part B

Part A

Part C

Ring

1. For each part, string the beads onto the head-pins. Cut the excess pin length and curl the tips into loops.

Refer to the Jewelry Making Technique Guide on pages 124-125 for detailed instructions on making headpin loops.

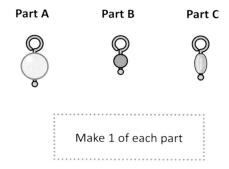

Part A   Part B   Part C

Make 1 of each part

2. Using flat-nose pliers, vertically open the headpin loops. Attach to the loop on the ring base, then close the headpin loops.

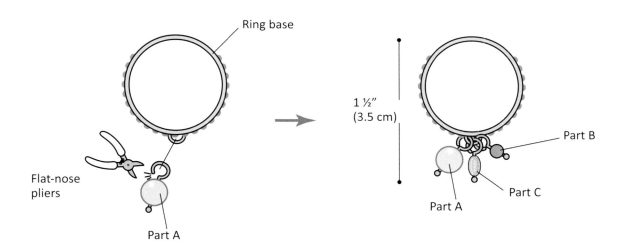

Ring base

1 ½"
(3.5 cm)

Flat-nose
pliers

Part A

Part A

Part B

Part C

KNOT GUIDE

Overhand Knot

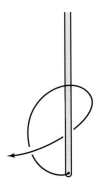

1. Make a loop. Bring the end through the loop.

2. Pull the end to close the loop.

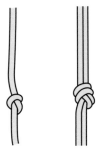

3. Completed view of the overhand knot. Follow the same process when using multiple strands.

Slip Knot

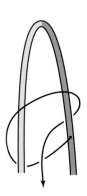

1. This knot can be tied with a single folded strand or with multiple strands. Use one strand to make a loop around the other, then bring the end through the loop. This is the same process as the overhand knot.

2. Pull the end to close the loop.

3. Completed view of the slip knot.

Beaded Brooch Bracelet

Shown on page 78

FINISHED SIZE

▶ Refer to the full-size templates for each project variation.

MATERIALS

Refer to the diagrams on pages 98 and 100-102 for suggested bead sizes, shapes, and colors.

▶ Assorted Czech glass beads
▶ Assorted seed beads
▶ Two 2" x 2" (5 x 5 cm) pieces of black felt
▶ 17 ¾" (45 cm) of ⅜" (10 mm) wide black ribbon
▶ One black ⅝" (16 mm) long pin back
▶ Sewing thread in coordinating colors to beads
▶ Jewelry and beading glue

TOOLS

▶ Extra-fine sewing needle (must be fine enough to fit through beads)

INSTRUCTIONS

1. Make a copy of the full-size template below. Cut out and trace the template onto the two pieces of felt. Cut out the two pieces of felt.

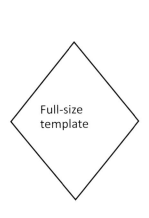

Full-size template

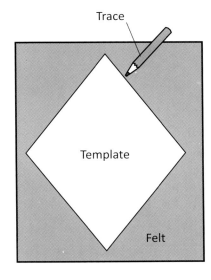

Trace

Template

Felt

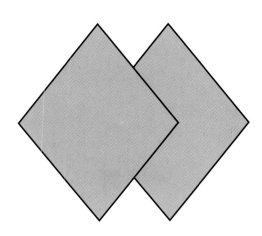

2. Sew the beads to one piece of felt following the diagram (see pages 100-102 for bead patterns of other brooch variations). Refer to the guide below for detailed instructions on sewing beads.

Diamond Brooch

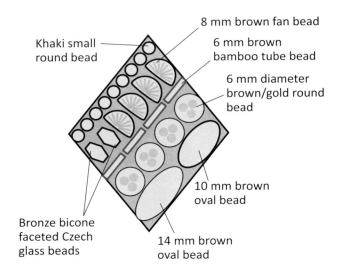

Khaki small round bead

8 mm brown fan bead

6 mm brown bamboo tube bead

6 mm diameter brown/gold round bead

10 mm brown oval bead

Bronze bicone faceted Czech glass beads

14 mm brown oval bead

*Use tortoise shell seed beads around the edges.

How to Sew Beads

Large Beads

1. Insert thread through eye of needle and knot

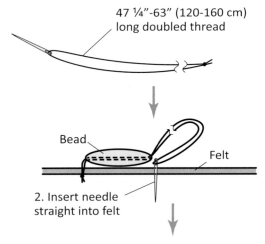

47 ¼"-63" (120-160 cm) long doubled thread

Bead

Felt

2. Insert needle straight into felt

3. Bring thread through bead twice before attaching next bead

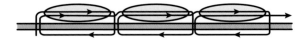

Small Beads

1. Bring thread through 5 beads at a time before inserting through felt

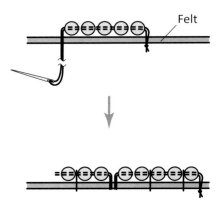

Felt

2. Stitch between every couple of beads to secure thread to felt

3. Sew the pin back to the other piece of felt. Glue the two pieces of felt with wrong sides together.

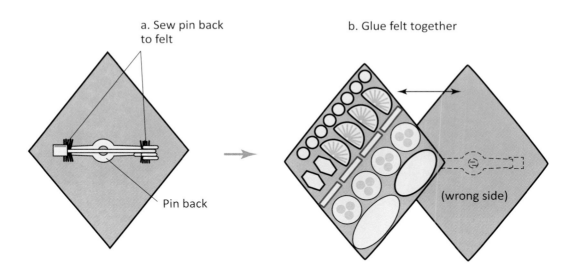

a. Sew pin back to felt

Pin back

b. Glue felt together

(wrong side)

4. Sew seed beads to the edges of the brooch. Refer to the guide on page 100 for detailed instructions. String the ribbon through the pin back on the back of brooch to complete the bracelet.

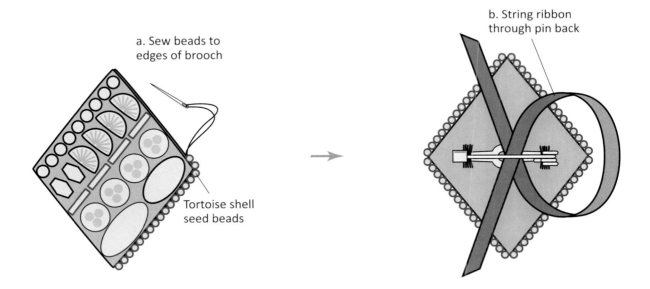

a. Sew beads to edges of brooch

Tortoise shell seed beads

b. String ribbon through pin back

How to Sew Beads to Brooch Edges

The following diagrams show one strand of thread for visual clarity. Use two strands of thread when sewing.

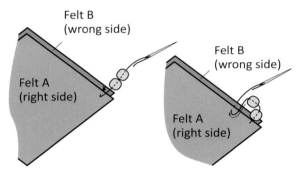 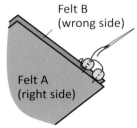 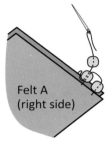 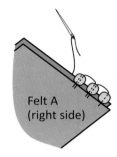

1. Make a knot at the end of the thread. Insert the needle through to the right side of Felt A. String two seed beads onto the needle.

2. Insert the needle through both pieces of felt and draw it out on the right side of Felt B.

3. Insert the needle through the second bead from the Felt A side to the Felt B side. Do not sew through the felt.

4. String another seed bead onto the needle.

5. Repeat steps 2-4 to sew beads around all edges of the brooch.

BEAD PATTERNS & TEMPLATES

Rectangle Brooch

10 x 15 mm clear purple triangular glass bead

Purple seed bead

15 beads

7 mm pink bicone faceted Czech glass bead

8 beads

5 mm matte pink donut-shaped beads

4 mm matte pink round Czech glass bead

5 mm clear purple square Czech glass bead

4 mm pink oval glass bead

10 beads

2 mm pink tube bead

Full-size template

*Use pink seed beads around the edges.

Heart Brooch

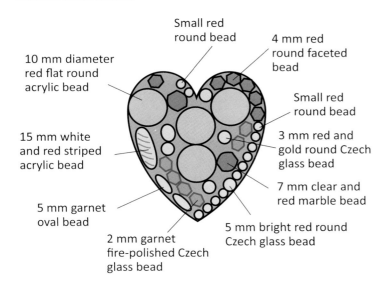

Small red round bead

4 mm red round faceted bead

10 mm diameter red flat round acrylic bead

Small red round bead

15 mm white and red striped acrylic bead

3 mm red and gold round Czech glass bead

7 mm clear and red marble bead

5 mm garnet oval bead

2 mm garnet fire-polished Czech glass bead

5 mm bright red round Czech glass bead

Full-size template

*Use red seed beads around the edges.

Oval Brooch

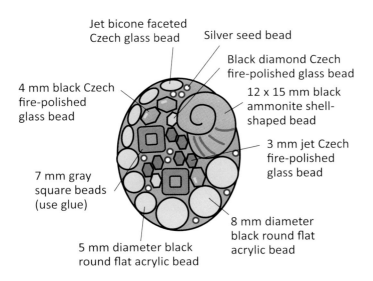

Jet bicone faceted Czech glass bead

Silver seed bead

Black diamond Czech fire-polished glass bead

4 mm black Czech fire-polished glass bead

12 x 15 mm black ammonite shell-shaped bead

3 mm jet Czech fire-polished glass bead

7 mm gray square beads (use glue)

8 mm diameter black round flat acrylic bead

5 mm diameter black round flat acrylic bead

Full-size template

*Use black seed beads around the edges.

Clover Brooch

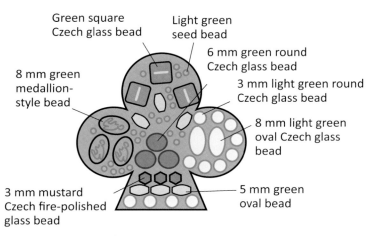

Green square
Czech glass bead

Light green
seed bead

6 mm green round
Czech glass bead

8 mm green
medallion-
style bead

3 mm light green round
Czech glass bead

8 mm light green
oval Czech glass
bead

3 mm mustard
Czech fire-polished
glass bead

5 mm green
oval bead

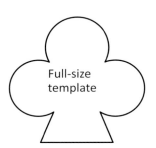

Full-size
template

*Use green seed beads around the edges.

Spade Brooch

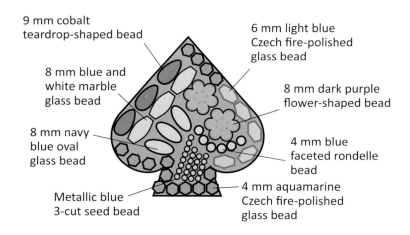

9 mm cobalt
teardrop-shaped bead

6 mm light blue
Czech fire-polished
glass bead

8 mm blue and
white marble
glass bead

8 mm dark purple
flower-shaped bead

8 mm navy
blue oval
glass bead

4 mm blue
faceted rondelle
bead

Metallic blue
3-cut seed bead

4 mm aquamarine
Czech fire-polished
glass bead

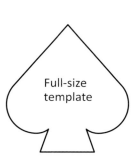

Full-size
template

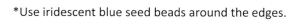

*Use iridescent blue seed beads around the edges.

---- 4. ----

Global Jewelry

Inspired by travels around the world, this collection combines bold colors and exotic designs. These bracelets are perfect for adding a punch of color to everyday life.

Winding Wire Bracelets & Choker

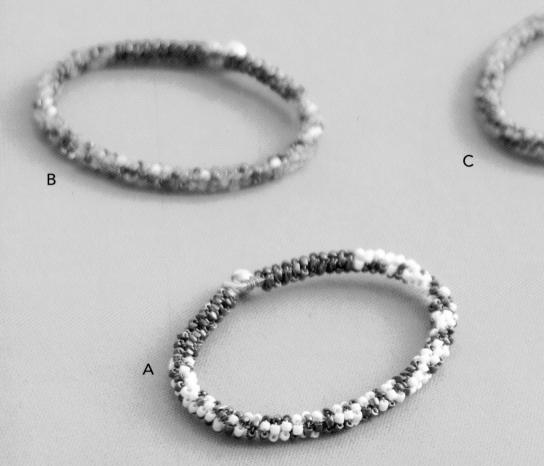

B

C

A

At first glance, these designs may appear braided, but they are actually composed of seed beads wound around a wire core. Use the color combinations shown here or mix and match to create your own unique variation.

Instructions on page 109

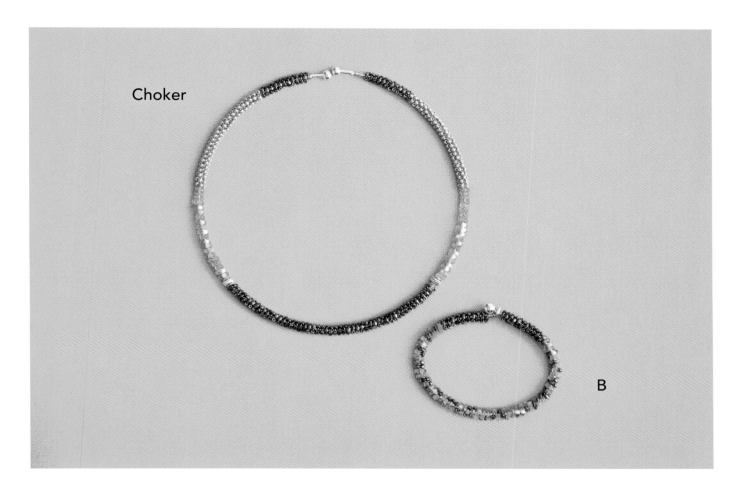

Choker

B

Bracelet B is designed to coordinate with the choker.

Wave Bracelets

A

B

Combine long and short beads to create this fluid, wave-shaped bracelet. This design uses the same construction technique as the Square Bead Wrap Bracelet on page 14, but has a completely different look due to the unique combination of beads.

Instructions on page 112

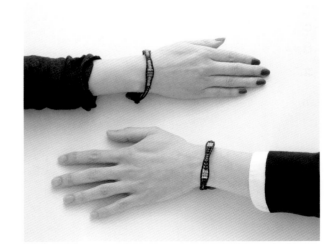

Woven Bead Cuffs

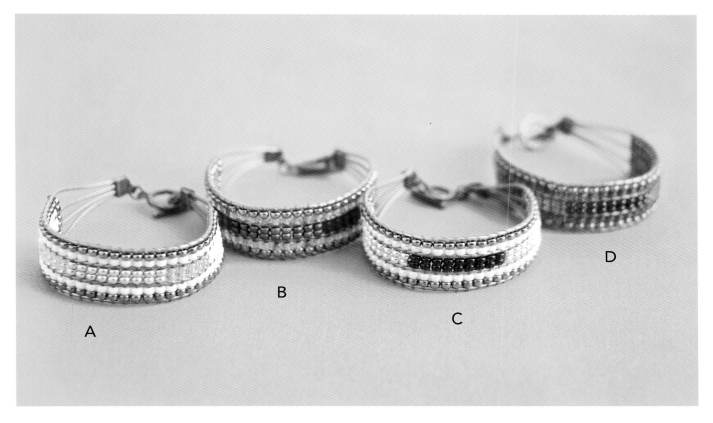

A

B

C

D

Weave seed beads onto four strands of leather cord using the ladder stitch technique. Seed beads are available in a wide variety of colors, making the design possibilities endless.

Instructions on page 114

Crystal Wrapped Bangles

For a quick yet stylish design, glue rhinestone chain to a bangle bracelet base, then wrap with embroidery floss. Use a single color for a chic bracelet or combine several shades for a festive look.

Instructions on page 116

19

Winding Wire Bracelets and Choker

Shown on page 104

FINISHED SIZE

- Bracelets: 7" (18 cm) long
- Choker: 14 ½" (37 cm) long

MATERIALS

White Bracelet (A)

- ▸ 130 white 3-cut round size 8 seed beads
- ▸ 250 bronze 3-cut round size 8 seed beads
- ▸ 78 ¾" (200 cm) of 28-gauge gold color brass wire
- ▸ One gold bangle bracelet base
- ▸ Jewelry and beading glue

Orange & Green Bracelet (B)

- ▸ 100 orange 3-cut round size 8 seed beads
- ▸ 185 bronze 3-cut round size 8 seed beads
- ▸ 95 bamboo green 3 mm seed beads
- ▸ 78 ¾" (200 cm) of 28-gauge gold color brass wire
- ▸ One gold bangle bracelet base
- ▸ Jewelry and beading glue

Turquoise Bracelet (C)

- ▸ 130 turquoise 3-cut round size 8 seed beads
- ▸ 250 bronze 3-cut round size 8 seed beads
- ▸ 78 ¾" (200 cm) of 28-gauge gold color brass wire
- ▸ One gold bangle bracelet base
- ▸ Jewelry and beading glue

Choker

- ▸ 340 bronze 3-cut round size 8 seed beads
- ▸ 40 orange 3-cut round size 8 seed beads
- ▸ 260 matte gold round size 8 seed beads
- ▸ 140 bamboo green 3 mm seed beads
- ▸ Two gold 5 mm barrel-shaped metal spacer beads
- ▸ One gold choker necklace base with end caps
- ▸ Jewelry and beading glue

INSTRUCTIONS

Bracelets

1. Wrap the wire around the bracelet base.

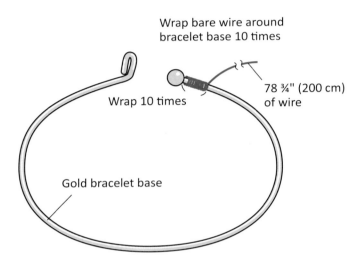

Wrap bare wire around
bracelet base 10 times

Wrap 10 times

78 ¾" (200 cm)
of wire

Gold bracelet base

2. String the beads onto the wire and wrap around the bracelet base.

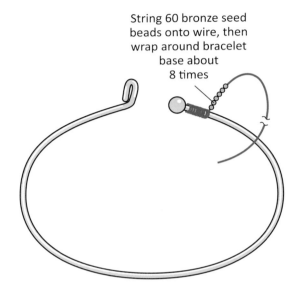

String 60 bronze seed
beads onto wire, then
wrap around bracelet
base about
8 times

3. Continue stringing the beads onto the wire and wrapping around the bracelet base. Refer to the chart for bead color combinations for the middle section of each bracelet variation. Refer to the photos on pages 104-105 for bead color placement.

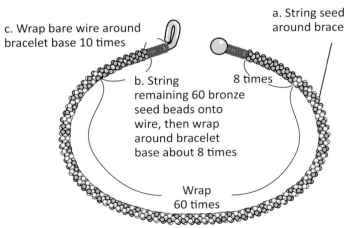

c. Wrap bare wire around
bracelet base 10 times

a. String seed beads onto wire, then wrap
around bracelet base 60 times

b. String
remaining 60 bronze
seed beads onto
wire, then wrap
around bracelet
base about 8 times

8 times

Wrap
60 times

BEAD COLOR COMBINATION CHART

A	130 white, 130 bronze
B	100 orange, 65 bronze, 95 bamboo green
C	130 turquoise, 130 bronze

Choker

Wrap the wire around the necklace base. String the beads onto the wire and wrap around the necklace base, alternating colors as indicated by the diagram.

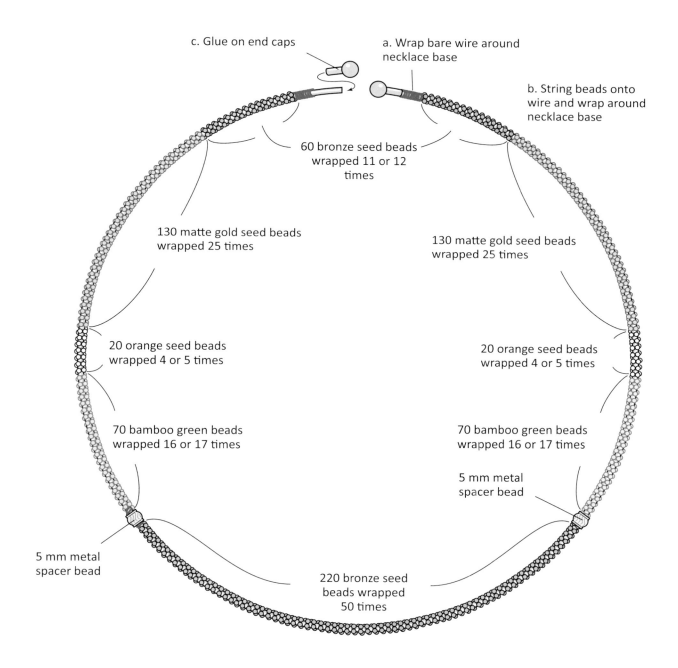

c. Glue on end caps

a. Wrap bare wire around necklace base

b. String beads onto wire and wrap around necklace base

60 bronze seed beads wrapped 11 or 12 times

130 matte gold seed beads wrapped 25 times

130 matte gold seed beads wrapped 25 times

20 orange seed beads wrapped 4 or 5 times

20 orange seed beads wrapped 4 or 5 times

70 bamboo green beads wrapped 16 or 17 times

70 bamboo green beads wrapped 16 or 17 times

5 mm metal spacer bead

5 mm metal spacer bead

220 bronze seed beads wrapped 50 times

Wave Bracelets

Shown on page 106

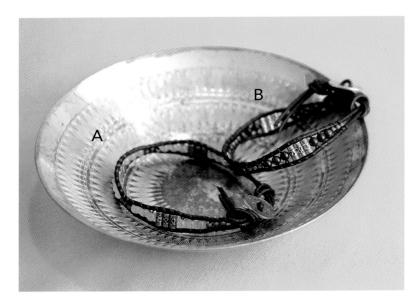

FINISHED SIZE

▸ About 9 ¾" (25 cm) long

MATERIALS

Yellow Bracelet (A)

▸ 18 4 mm round yellow quartz beads
▸ 12 large brass seed beads
▸ Nine brass 7 mm tube-shaped spacer beads
▸ One brass ⅝" (16.5 mm) diameter button
▸ 27 ½" (70 cm) of 2 mm round black leather cord
▸ 78 ¾" (200 cm) of black monofilament cord

Blue Bracelet (B)

▸ 18 4 mm round lapis lazuli beads
▸ 12 large brass seed beads
▸ Nine brass 7 mm tube-shaped spacer beads
▸ One brass ⅝" (16.5 mm) diameter button
▸ 27 ½" (70 cm) of 2 mm round black leather cord
▸ 78 ¾" (200 cm) of black monofilament cord

TOOLS

▸ Beading needle

INSTRUCTIONS

Follow the same process used to make the Square Bead Wrap Bracelet, as shown in the Technique Overview on pages 23-25.

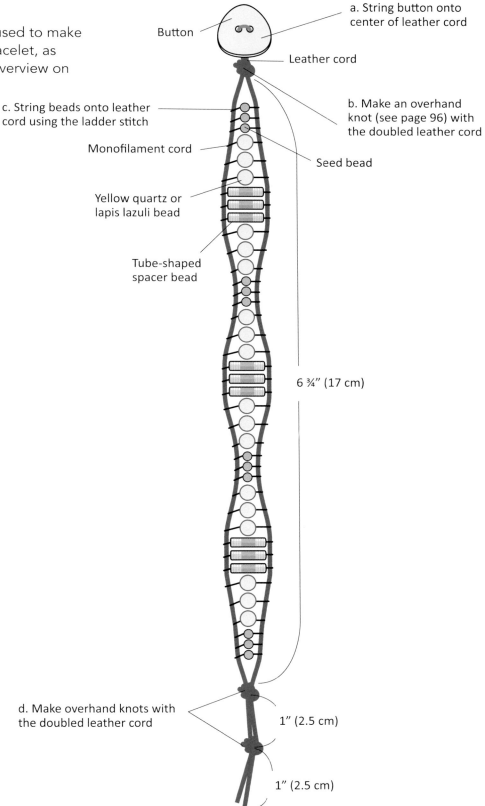

Button

a. String button onto center of leather cord

Leather cord

c. String beads onto leather cord using the ladder stitch

b. Make an overhand knot (see page 96) with the doubled leather cord

Monofilament cord

Seed bead

Yellow quartz or lapis lazuli bead

Tube-shaped spacer bead

6 ¾" (17 cm)

d. Make overhand knots with the doubled leather cord

1" (2.5 cm)

1" (2.5 cm)

21 Woven Bead Cuffs

Shown on page 107

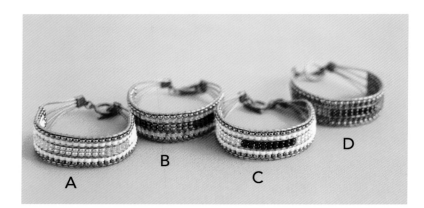

A B C D

FINISHED SIZE

▸ About 7 ¼" (18.5 cm) long

MATERIALS

Refer to the Color Combination Chart for each bracelet variation.

▸ 3 mm round seed beads
  • 70 bronze
  • 78 Color A
  • 20 Color B
  • 18 Color C
▸ Eight brass 4.5 mm jump rings
▸ Two brass 6 mm crimp beads

▸ One brass toggle clasp
▸ 39 ½" (100 cm) of 1.2 mm round bronze leather cord
▸ 118 ¼" (300 cm) of brown monofilament cord

TOOLS

▸ Beading needle
▸ Flat-nose pliers

COLOR COMBINATION CHART

	A	B	C	D
Color A	Off-white	Light green	White	Magenta
Color B	Bright yellow	Bright green	Silver	Light purple
Color C	Gold	Iridescent green	Brown	Iridescent purple

INSTRUCTIONS

Cut the leather cord into two 19 ¾" (50 cm) long pieces and fold in half. Using the ladder stitch technique shown on pages 23-25, attach the beads to the leather cord using two strands of monofilament cord. Trim the excess leather cord and attach crimp beads to both ends of the bracelet using flat-nose pliers. Attach jump rings and toggle clasp components to both ends of the bracelet.

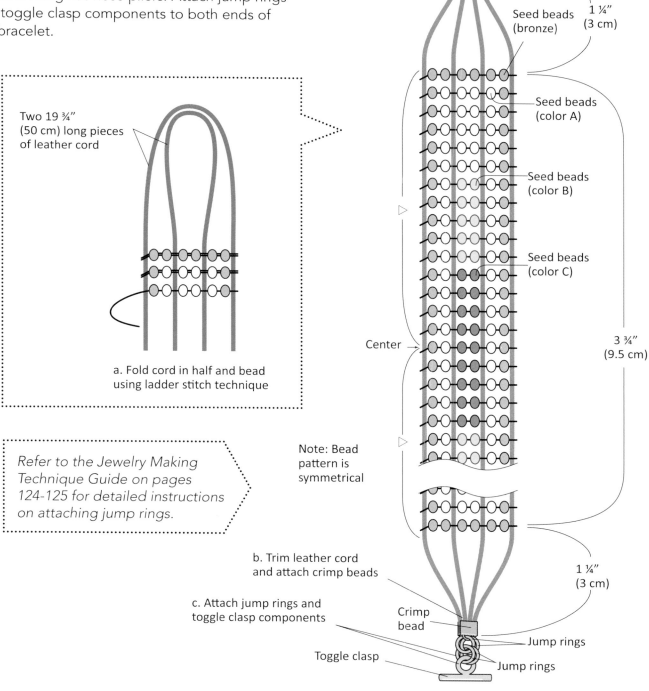

Two 19 ¾" (50 cm) long pieces of leather cord

a. Fold cord in half and bead using ladder stitch technique

Refer to the Jewelry Making Technique Guide on pages 124-125 for detailed instructions on attaching jump rings.

Note: Bead pattern is symmetrical

Toggle clasp

c.

Jump rings

Jump rings

Crimp bead
b.

1 ¼"
(3 cm)

Seed beads (bronze)

Seed beads (color A)

Seed beads (color B)

Seed beads (color C)

Center

3 ¾"
(9.5 cm)

b. Trim leather cord and attach crimp beads

c. Attach jump rings and toggle clasp components

Toggle clasp

Crimp bead

1 ¼"
(3 cm)

Jump rings

Jump rings

22 Crystal Wrapped Bangles

Shown on page 108

FINISHED SIZE

▸ Refer to diagram on page 118

MATERIALS

Black Bracelet

▸ 5 ½" (14 cm) of 4 mm black diamond rhinestone cupchain
▸ One ½" (12 mm) wide gold bangle bracelet base
▸ 338 ¾" (860 cm) of black DMC No. 25 embroidery floss
▸ Jewelry and beading glue

Multicolor Bracelet

▸ 5 ¼" (13 cm) of 4 mm black diamond rhinestone cupchain
▸ One ½" (12 mm) wide gold bangle bracelet base
▸ 79" (190 cm) each of white and gray DMC No. 25 embroidery floss
▸ 59" (150 cm) each of yellow, pink, blue, and green DMC No. 25 embroidery floss
▸ Jewelry and beading glue

INSTRUCTIONS

Black Bracelet

1. Glue the cupchain to the center of the bangle bracelet base.

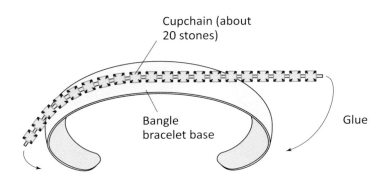

Cupchain (about 20 stones)

Bangle bracelet base

Glue

2. Wrap the embroidery floss around the bangle bracelet base.

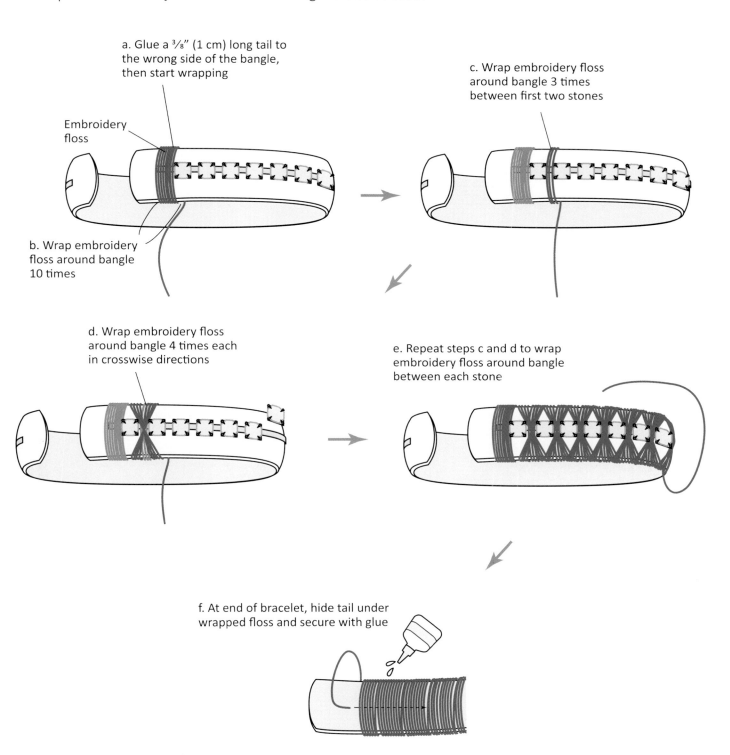

a. Glue a ³⁄₈" (1 cm) long tail to the wrong side of the bangle, then start wrapping

c. Wrap embroidery floss around bangle 3 times between first two stones

Embroidery floss

b. Wrap embroidery floss around bangle 10 times

d. Wrap embroidery floss around bangle 4 times each in crosswise directions

e. Repeat steps c and d to wrap embroidery floss around bangle between each stone

f. At end of bracelet, hide tail under wrapped floss and secure with glue

Multicolor Bracelet

Follow the same process used for the Black Bracelet (see pages 116-117), but follow the diagram below for floss color pattern. To change colors, tie the old color and new color together with 2-3 knots on the wrong side of the bangle. Cover the knots when wrapping the new color around the bracelet.

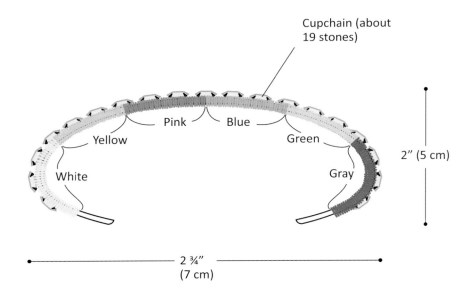

Cupchain (about 19 stones)

Pink   Blue

Yellow   Green

White   Gray

2" (5 cm)

2 ¾"
(7 cm)

Wrap Bracelet
Tips & Tricks

BRACELET COMBINATIONS

The designs included in this book are meant to be mixed and matched to achieve the stylish layered look. Here are a few suggestions of designs that work well together. Have fun experimenting with your own combinations!

A WALK IN THE WOODS

Green is the predominant color in this collection of bead and fabric bracelets. Use a floral print fabric to tie the look together.

Bracelets:

Winding Wire Bracelet (page 109),
Woven Fabric Bracelet (page 63), and
Woven Bead Cuff (page 114)

AT THE REGATTA

Combine bracelets in a classic blue and white color scheme for a nautical feel. A metal sailboat charm completes the look.

Bracelets:

Braided Friendship Bracelet (page 50),
Square Bead Wrap Bracelet (page 23), and
Nautical Wrap Bracelet (page 30)

SUMMERTIME PICNIC

A classic red, white, and blue color scheme lends a summery look to this collection of bracelets.

Bracelets:

Square Bead Wrap Bracelet (page 23),
Beaded Square Knot Bracelet (page 55), and
Woven Fabric Bracelet (page 63)

AN AFTERNOON OF SHOPPING WITH FRIENDS

Combine elegant rhinestone and chiffon with more rustic materials like turquoise and leather for the perfect blend of casual style.

Bracelets:

Square Knot Rope Amulet (page 66), Sparkling Chiffon Bracelet (page 34), and Simple Wrap Bracelet (page 39)

AN EVENING AT THE OPERA

This elegant look is created by combining glamorous materials like pearls and rhine-stones. The black color scheme makes this suitable for a formal occasion.

Bracelets:

Square Knot Rope Amulet (page 66), Cotton Pearl Bracelet (page 87), and Crystal Wrapped Bangle (page 116)

A GIFT FOR HIM

When worked in a masculine color scheme such as the black, navy, and turquoise shown here, many designs are suitable for men.

Bracelets:

Wave Bracelet (page 112), Turquoise Bracelet (page 84), and Convertible Braid Bracelet (page 69)

SIMPLE WRAP BRACELETS

Make a few quick and easy wrap bracelets to complement more ornately beaded designs and achieve a layered look. Use silk ribbon or shiny elastic tape in coordinating colors with your other bracelets. Add metal charms to complete the look.

SILK RIBBON WRAP BRACELETS

Hand dyed silk ribbon is available in beautiful, one-of-a-kind variegated colors. String a metal charm onto a length of ribbon, then tie around your wrist as shown on page 123.

A silk ribbon wrap bracelet layered with the Square Bead Wrap Bracelet from page 23

ELASTIC TAPE

Shiny elastic tape also works well for simple wrap bracelets. Attach a metal charm and loop the elastic twice before knotting.

An elastic tape wrap bracelet layered with the Woven Bead Cuff from page 114

HOW TO TIE SIMPLE WRAP BRACELETS

Follow these steps to tie simple wrap bracelets around your wrist.

Single Strand Wrap

1. Hold one end of the ribbon between your thumb and index finger. Wrap the ribbon around your wrist several times.

2. Tie the two ends together.

3. Pull the ends to hide the knot under the wraps.

4. Wind the ends around the wraps a few times.

Double Wrap

1. Fold the ribbon in half and position on top of your wrist. If using a charm, align the charm at the center of your arm.

2. Bring the ribbon ends through the folded loop from step 1.

3. Wrap the doubled ribbon around your wrist several times.

4. Tie the two ends together and pull the ends to hide the knot under the wraps (steps 2 and 3 above). Wind the ends around the wraps a few times.

JEWELRY MAKING TECHNIQUE GUIDE

Pin Loops

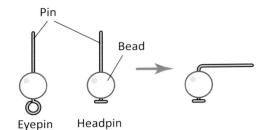

Pin
Bead
Eyepin   Headpin

¼"
(6-7 mm)

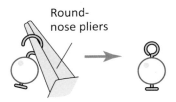

Round-
nose pliers

1. String a bead onto the pin. Using round-nose pliers, bend the pin at a 90° angle.

2. Trim the pin about ¼" (6-7 mm) from the bead.

3. Grasp the end of the pin with round-nose pliers. Rotate the pliers to curl the end of the pin around the tip of the pliers. Note: When connecting the pin loop to other components, follow the same process used for attaching jump rings, as shown on page 125.

Cord Ends

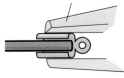

Flat-nose pliers

1. Use flat-nose pliers to squeeze the cord end around the cord.

2. Apply a small dab of glue to secure the cord end in place.

Jump Rings

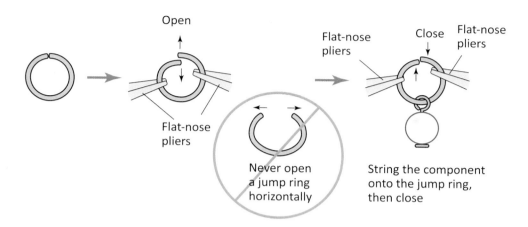

Open

Flat-nose pliers

Flat-nose pliers

Close

Flat-nose pliers

Never open a jump ring horizontally

String the component onto the jump ring, then close

Always open and close jump rings vertically using flat-nose pliers. If you open the ring horizontally, you will deform the shape of the jump ring. Refer to step 5 on page 83 for photos of opening and closing jump rings properly.

Bead Tips

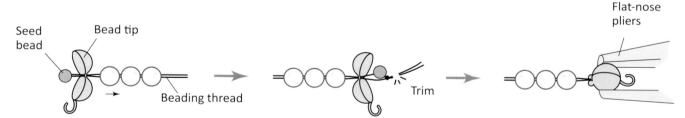

Seed bead

Bead tip

Beading thread

Trim

Flat-nose pliers

1. To start, string a seed bead onto the center of a piece of beading thread and fold in half. Thread the bead tip and remaining beads onto the doubled thread.

2. To finish, string a bead tip onto the doubled thread. String a seed bead onto one strand and knot 5-6 times. Trim the excess thread.

3. Use flat-nose pliers to close both bead tips around the seed beads.

Resources

UNITED STATES

BEADSHOP.COM

Huge selection of beads and stringing materials including Czech glass beads
www.beadshop.com

FIRE MOUNTAIN GEMS

Online bead emporium
www.firemountaingems.com

FUSION BEADS

Online bead shop
www.fusionbeads.com

JO-ANN FABRICS

National craft store selling beads, wire, thread, and tools
www.joann.com

MICHAELS

National craft store with great selection of beading supplies
www.michaels.com

RIO GRANDE

Wide assortment of tools, beading supplies, and jewelry findings
www.riogrande.com

UNITED KINGDOM

BEADS DIRECT

Online bead retailer based in the UK
www.beadsdirect.co.uk

BEADS UNLIMITED

UK-based website for beading tools and materials
www.beadsunlimited.co.uk

BEADWORKS

Wide range of semi-precious beads and high quality findings
www.beadworks.co.uk

HOBBYCRAFT

Largest arts and crafts retailer in the UK
www.hobbycraft.co.uk

AUSTRALIA

BEADS ONLINE

Offers beads, pendants, charms, findings, and tools
www.beadsonline.com.au

BEADS N CRYSTALS

Great selection of beading supplies and tools
www.beadsncrystals.com.au

THAT BEAD SHOP

Online only bead shop offering beads, pendants, and findings
www.thatbeadshop.com.au

About the Author

Keiko Sakamoto worked as a floral designer for over 10 years before launching her jewelry business. In 1999, she opened her shop called Beads Cafe. Her vision was to a create place where people could learn jewelry making in a relaxed setting similar to a cafe. Sakamoto's work has been featured on television and in magazines.